The Haggadah About Nothing

The (Unofficial) Seinfeld Haggadah

Rabbi Sam Reinstein

© Samuel Reinstein
All Rights Reserved
ISBN: 978-0-578-83282-1

Hebrew text adapted from Sefaria.org
Illustrations: Shira Greenspan
Typesetting: James Conway

Seinfeld Logo: Trademark owned by Castle Rock Entertainment and Sony Pictures., Public domain, via Wikimedia Commons.
Apartment photo sourced from WENN Rights Ltd / Alamy Stock Photo.
Short Seinfeld excerpts sourced from http://seinfeldscripts.com/ used for commentary/parody purposes only

All rights to the artwork reserved by Shira Greenspan

To Susan Ross:
Her death takes place in the shadow of new life.
She's not really dead if we find a way to remember her.
-Jerry Seinfeld

This page was intentionally left blank.
All the other pages are about something. This page is about nothing.

The Airing of Acknowledgements

The tradition of published books begins with the airing of acknowledgements. I got a lot of blessings from you people. Now, you're gonna hear about it.

To Jerry Seinfeld and Larry David: Thank you for creating the show that inspired this Haggadah. Not only is Seinfeld hilarious, but it also provides insights into the nature of being human. Watching Seinfeld was as much a learning experience for me as it makes me laugh.

To Congregation Kol Israel, my spiritual home in Brooklyn.

To James Conway who formatted the Haggadah, Sruly Heller who edited the Divrei Torah, and Shira Greenspan who made the illustrations.

To Eli Lebowicz, comedian extraordinaire, who served as an excellent sounding board throughout this process.

To Kivi Geller who introduced me to Seinfeld in the dorms of Yeshiva University.

To the West Hempstead Reinsteins, and in particular to Aunt Gila A"H, who hosted my family for many Pesach holidays, helping instill in me a love for the holiday and the Seder.

To David Dreyfus A"H, who always showed that you can never be doing too many things at once.

To my four grandparents: Samuel and Margot Lauber and Edith and Yoseph Reinstein who sacrificed everything to give my parents a better life in America in the aftermath of the Holocaust. They are looking down probably confused, but also hopefully amazed and proud that only two generations after spending Passover in concentration camps, their grandson wrote a Haggadah based on a critically acclaimed comedy written by two Jews.

To my parents, Esther Lauber and Rabbi Alvin Reinstein, who have done more than I can express on this page.

To my sister, Margot, who was a great cheerleader from Israel and serves as a great example of how modernity and Torah interact that this book represents. (and Thank you to her husband Josh and their children: Yoshi, Boaz, and Rafi)

To my two babies, Miriam and Sophia, who lived through much of this book's creation. I'll cherish the memories of those late night feeds and holding you both in the carrier while typing and researching.

To my son, Leo, whose bright energy has been so important during this past year. Thank you for sharing my love of Torah (and television) with me. Yes, Helloooo and I know those pretzels are making you thirsty.

To Hannah, my wife, who accomplished the real feats of strength during the writing of this Haggadah. Thank you for supporting me throughout this process, and for not giving up on me when I started speaking purely in Seinfeld references and puns.

Introduction

Seinfeld: The Finale (S09E24)
JERRY: See now, to me, that button is in the worst possible spot.
GEORGE: Really?
JERRY: Oh yeah. The second button is the key button. It literally makes or breaks the shirt. Look at it, it's too high, it's in no-man's land.
GEORGE: Haven't we had this conversation before?
JERRY: You think?
GEORGE: I think we have.
JERRY: Yeah, maybe we have.

END

What's the deal with a *Seinfeld* themed Haggadah?

Seinfeld's popularity, on the most basic level, perfectly complements the Pesach story. *Seinfeld* changed TV sitcoms for the better and in the minds of many, including a host of media, defined modern television thereafter. Its lasting impact traveled far beyond its nine seasons and is still very much felt today. It became the paradigmatic TV show and retained a quintessential character unique to any other similarly epochal show.

The Pesach story, in a different way, meets similar acclaim. The story of the Exodus is as iconic as it gets. The Seder is one of Judaism's most widely kept traditions, and the Shema, with its invocation to remembering the Exodus the Seder celebrates, is one of Judaism's most well-known prayers. We invoke the Exodus when we say Kiddush on Friday night, and in the prayers when we go to sleep and wake up. The story is utilized throughout secular culture as well, especially in the United States. The iconic splitting of the Red Sea was in fact almost the Great Seal of the United States. (Benjamin Franklin wanted the seal to be of the splitting of the sea, while Thomas Jefferson wanted the children of Israel led by a cloud and pillar of fire.) When people are trying to free themselves from tyrannical rule, they hail the singularly iconic Exodus story, recorded in the Torah, that tells of the Jews leaving Egypt.

At the same time, *Seinfeld* may seem to be a resolutely unlikely Haggadah candidate. Defined by the creators as a "show about nothing[C1]," *Seinfeld* is largely concerned with the utterly mundane events in the characters' otherwise wildly New York lives. Going to get Chinese food[C2], getting stuck in a parking garage[C3], or getting frozen yogurt[C4] are adventures and narratives whose recounting would seem a far cry from the tales of God miraculously taking the Jewish people out of Egypt.

Beyond those surface contrasts however, *Seinfeld* and the Seder share similar messages in exactly the ways they seem starkly different. The Seder is supposed to change us. We are not supposed to view the Exodus as a one time event that happened to our ancestors, but rather as a process that transforms us on Seder night. In *Ha Lachma Anya* we proclaim, "this year we are slaves, next year we will be free people." We are supposed to view ourselves as slaves trying to escape the shackles of back-breaking labor. We similarly say, "In every generation a person must regard themselves as though they personally had gone out of Egypt." We are to view ourselves as if we are being freed from our own individual bondage on Pesach, not merely reliving some past experience. The structure of the Seder itself implores us to make this paradigm shift from our personal bondage to freedom. While there is an argument between Rav and Shmuel (Pesachim 116a) if the Seder is the spiritual journey or the physical one, the message is clear: you are supposed to experience the Haggadah's journey on Seder night for yourself and change for the better.

Rav Kook, the first Ashkenazi Chief Rabbi of Israel, notices a change of language style in Nirtzah, the last section of the Haggadah. Nirtzah, literally translated as "it was accepted" is written in the passive voice, while all other parts of the Haggadah are written in the active voice. We take out the matza, wash our hands, say Hallel — all active prompts except the last step of the Seder. Rav Kook notes that we have undergone a significant transformation over the Seder night. We are not the same people who started the night; we are, rather, elevated spiritually. Through all the Seder's actions, we have attained a higher level of freedom and holiness. At Seder's end, we are ready to sing, ready to accept the Almighty. We have changed and no longer need to be actively prompted to do so — "it was accepted" already.

Seinfeld, as a show and an ethos, could not seem more different. The characters never change — they remain resolutely static in their manners, habits, and patterns. In just about every episode, the characters revert back to how they were at the beginning, with no meaningful shift in their lives. Even when some differences persist — a girlfriend, a job, a joke — the characters themselves never change. Other than the few episodes of "The Pilot[C5]," virtually no storyline lasts past one episode.

This was not an accident. Larry David, the TV show's co-creator alongside Jerry Seinfeld, constantly repeated a sacred mantra to the writing team: "no hugging, no learning." Jerry, George, Elaine, and Kramer were never written to evolve or designed to change. The main characters were manifestly self-absorbed, obsessed with minor details to levels of emotionally corrosive pedantry and altogether abhorrent. They are akin to Plato's fixed essences; beauty is beauty, and a chair is a chair, Jerry is Jerry, and Elaine is Elaine. Nothing ever really changes.

The best example of this are the scenes that open and close the entire series. The last conversation, quoted at the beginning of this essay, seems random at first glance. Shirt Buttons? Why are they going on about shirt buttons? When you realize it echoes the exact same conversation they had during the first scene of the pilot, it makes a lot more sense. They have just gone through nine years of adventures, endured a trial that landed them in prison for a year, and yet have the same exact meaningless conversation. When you watch *Seinfeld*, you spend nine years getting to know the characters. Over time, you likely begin to relate to the characters, and understandably so. The stories are relatable to the banalities of our lives. In countless situations, Jerry and the gang act in terrible fashion in ways we secretly wish we could emulate, if it was not for society's expectations, or knew we could if we were not as civil, not as bound to society's rules. The show lulls you into thinking you are somewhat like the four lead characters, only to pull the carpet out under you during "The

Finale[C6]." "The Finale" parades the central characters' misdeed after misdeed, culminating in a jury's decision to imprison the four leads for low quality of character. We spend nine seasons thinking we are the New York four, only to realize we are really the jury deciding that their inability to change is the antithesis of being a good citizen.

In "The Pilot[C7]," George gives meta commentary on the show calling it a "show about nothing," — it is, in actuality, anything but. We see what nine years of "nothing" really looks like, forcing us to consider if a life without forward progress is worth living. *Seinfeld* shows that a life of "something" is the only real option.

Rav Yosef Dov Soleveitchik, luminary of the American Modern Orthodox movement, explains that the purpose of the Exodus and thereby its remembrance is that it is supposed to teach "...ethical sensitivity, what it truly means to be a Jew. It sought to transform the Jew into a rachaman, one possessing a heightened form of ethical sensitivity and responsiveness." The *Seinfeld* characters never do that — they never transform. On Pesach, we seek to learn the lesson of *Seinfeld*. If we don't stop and examine the shackles we place on ourselves, we will never be free. If we do not engage with our personal histories in a serious way, we will never move forward. The four main characters never learn and they end up in prison. Through the Seder, may we change for the better so that "now we are slaves, next year may we be free."

THE HAGGADAH ABOUT NOTHING

Preparations for Passover

On the night before Seder night (or Thursday night if Passover starts Saturday night) we search for chametz throughout the house. It is customary to place ten pieces of bread throughout the house before the search. Say the blessing before the search.

Blessed are You, Lord our God, King of the universe, who made us holy with His commandments, and commanded us to remove the leaven.

The search is conducted. After the search say the blessing:

Any leaven that may still be in the house, which I have not seen or have not removed shall be as if it does not exist, and as the dust of the earth.

═══ BEE BA DO DUM DUM, BUM BADUM BUM BUH, BAH DUH, BAH DAH DUM DUM, DUM DEDUM DUM DUM DUM DUM. BADA DO DUM DEDUM. ═══

The Chametz Break-Up

Jerry treats his girlfriends the way Jews treat chametz (leaven) before Pesach. A major recurring theme in the show is the main characters' dating lives, particularly the lead, Jerry Seinfeld. Jerry dates many women and has many girlfriends throughout *Seinfeld*. While it is debatable how you define "girlfriend" in the show, by my count Jerry has 66 girlfriends during the 180 episodes. Jerry is fickle with the women he dates and breaks up with them for minor reasons. This includes, but is by no means limited to, "faults" such as having "man hands[C8]," an annoying laugh[C9], eating her peas one at a time[C10], liking a Dockers commercial[C11], looking different in different lighting[C12], being "too good[C13]," shushing him while he's watching TV[C14], used a toothbrush that fell into the toilet[C15] and a variety of other perceived offenses. The conclusion is always the same: whenever Jerry finds a problem with a woman, she must be out.

Chametz on Pesach is treated like no other item in Jewish law. On the night before Pesach, we search our homes by candlelight

6 — PREPARATIONS

THE (UNOFFICIAL) SEINFELD HAGGADAH

הֲכָנוֹת לְפֶסַח

On the night before Seder night (or Thursday night if Passover starts Saturday night) we search for chametz throughout the house. It is customary to place ten pieces of bread throughout the house before the search. Say the blessing before the search.

בָּרוּךְ אַתָּה ה' אֱלֹהֵינוּ מֶלֶךְ הָעוֹלָם, אֲשֶׁר קִדְּשָׁנוּ בְּמִצְוֹתָיו, וְצִוָּנוּ עַל בִּעוּר חָמֵץ.

The search is conducted. After the search say the blessing:

כָּל חֲמִירָא וַחֲמִיעָא דְּאִכָּא בִרְשׁוּתִי, דְּלָא חֲמִתֵּהּ וּדְלָא בְעַרְתֵּהּ וּדְלָא יְדַעְנָא לֵהּ, לִבָּטֵיל וְלֶהֱוֵי הֶפְקֵר כְּעַפְרָא דְאַרְעָא.

בִּי בָּה דוּ דוּם דוּם, בּוּם בְּדוּם בּוּם בּוּ, בָּה דוּ, בָּה דָה דוּם דוּם, דוּם דְּדוּם דוּם דוּם דוּם דוּם. בָּדָה דוּ דוּם דְּדוּם.

to make sure that we are completely free of chametz. Not only may chametz not be eaten on Pesach, it may not be owned during the holiday and no benefit may be derived from chametz throughout the duration of Pesach. If you do own chametz on Pesach, you are not allowed to use it after the holiday. Most uniquely, chametz is not nullified (batel) in any quantity, unlike other objects and substances in Jewish law. (Normally things can be nullified if they are in a mixture.) Chametz is zero sum. Most Ashkenazim do not eat kitniyot, legumes, which may have either been mixed with tiny amounts of wheat or resemble wheat themselves, creating the potential for confusion. Even with substances not scripturally forbidden on Pesach, the prohibition is taken very seriously. Why are we so much

THE HAGGADAH ABOUT NOTHING

The next morning, we take all the chametz that was collected to be burned. Say the following at the burning:

Any leaven that may still be in the house, which I have or have not seen, which I have or have not removed, shall be as if it does not exist, and as the dust of the earth.

━━ BEE BA DO DUM DUM, BUM BADUM BUM BUH, BAH DUH, BAH DAH DUM DUM, DUM DEDUM DUM DUM DUM DUM. BADA DO DUM DEDUM. ━━

more strict about chametz on Pesach, both in manner and degree than with so much else of the tradition?

Pesach is the start of the Jewish people's relationship with God as a nation. As time goes on in the relationship, there is a place for our imperfections, but right at the beginning, the relationship is fragile and needs to be in a bubble (just like the bubble boy[C16]). Foreign things don't have a place at the beginning of a relationship, since it isn't strong enough yet. This is how I have understood Nadav and Avihu's (the Biblical Aaron's sons) punishment of death for bringing a "foreign fire" in the Mishkan (Tabernacle) during its inauguration, which we always read right before Pesach. They were punished so severely not only for what they did, but when they did it. The Mishkan was brand new, a new way for the Jewish people to relate to the Almighty. That relationship was not ready for a foreign fire, no matter how well meaning it was.

Jerry, in his relationships, never moves beyond the intensity of Pesach. He finds minor flaws in those he dates and treats them like they are chametz, or a foreign fire. But Pesach is only one week of the year. After Pesach, we can proceed beyond the blossoming stage of a relationship and exist without a bubble (unlike the bubble boy[*8]). Jerry never evolves to understand that even if the conditions of a relationship should be close to perfect at the beginning, it can, and must, move past that stage. The relationship's essence must always be about the people involved and not every detail.

Then again, Jerry having a healthy long-lasting relationship would probably not be quite as funny.

The Chametz Burning

Burning is a very specific way to destroy our chametz before Pesach. While there is the opinion of the Chachamim (a group of Rabbis) that you can "burn" your chametz in other ways — like

THE (UNOFFICIAL) SEINFELD HAGGADAH

The next morning, we take all the chametz that was collected to be burned. Say the following at the burning:

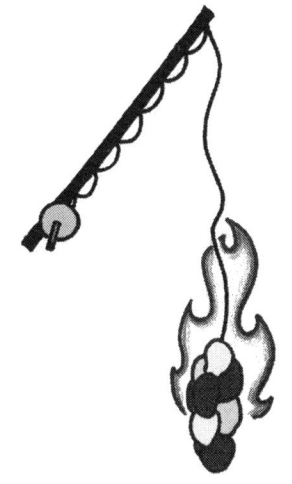

כָּל חֲמִירָא וַחֲמִיעָא דְּאִכָּא בִרְשׁוּתִי, דַּחֲזִתֵּהּ וּדְלָא חֲזִתֵּהּ, דַּחֲמִתֵּהּ וּדְלָא חֲמִתֵּהּ, דְּבַעַרְתֵּהּ וּדְלָא בִעַרְתֵּהּ, לִבָּטֵיל וְלֶהֱוֵי הֶפְקֵר כְּעַפְרָא דְאַרְעָא.

בִּי בה דו דום דום, בום בדום בום בו, בה דו, בה דה דום דום, דום דדום דום דום דום דום. בדה דו דום דדום.

throwing it into the sea, or more apropos to today, into the toilet — it is optimal to actually burn the chametz if possible.

Fire is unique because it reacts differently in different situations. Fires can easily be destructive — they can burn down houses or even metastasize into wildfires. A burning iron can burn George's beautiful hands[C17], instantly ending his hand model career. Concurrently, fire can transform an object in a positive or constructive way. It can forge metal, and it can bring raw food to an edible state. Even fires in fields can be either destructive or transformational. A hot fire can burn down an entire year of crops, but a "cold" fire can be lit in a controlled way to get rid of undergrowth and yield new crops.

In the Pesach story, we see the double nature of fire. A pillar of fire is what leads the Jewish people at night as they are leaving Egypt and fire is used to roast the Pesach sacrifice. At the same time, the Midrash, a large set of Rabbinic teachings, tells us that the hail that fell as the seventh of the ten plagues had fire inside making the downpour far more destructive.

In "The Bubble Boy[C18]" and subsequent "The Cheever Letters[C19]," we see the double nature of fire as well. Kramer uses fire to light a cigar but also leaves an unattended flame that burns down Susan's family built cabin. The only thing left after the cabin fire is a metal box, which Susan opens to discover love letters written to her father, Henry, by John Cheever, an American writer.

While the fire was obviously destructive, it also exposed the truth

הכנות — 9

of her father's relationship. Even though he spoke of the cabin a lot before the fire, the Cheever letters make the important cabin a mere afterthought. The cabin is destroyed, but the cabin is physical and ephemeral — Henry's relationship with John Cheever lives on and is perhaps even stronger for it. The fire uncovers who Henry really is by exposing the relationship, not his father's legacy of a cabin. Fire has a way of exposing the essence of the object. Cooking food with fire makes it actually become the food, intense fire makes the iron into a tool.

═ BEE BA DO DUM DUM, BUM BADUM BUM BUH, BAH DUH, BAH DAH DUM DUM, DUM DEDUM DUM DUM DUM DUM. BADA DO DUM DEDUM. ═

If the first day of Passover falls on Friday (or also on Thursday outside of Israel) the following is said before Passover begins over a cooked and baked (frequently matzah) item, which is then saved and eaten on Shabbat.

Blessed are You, Lord our God, King of the universe, who made us holy with His commandments, and commanded us concerning the Eruv.

═ BEE BA DO DUM DUM, BUM BADUM BUM BUH, BAH DUH, BAH DAH DUM DUM, DUM DEDUM DUM DUM DUM DUM. BADA DO DUM DEDUM. ═

The Helen Custom

There aren't too many explicit Jewish stereotypes in *Seinfeld*, but Helen, Jerry's mother, definitely fits the bill of a stereotypical "Jewish mother." Helen is protective of Jerry, ever-watchful from her post down in Florida. She says instantly, if not ominously, that she will "make a few calls" when she hears Crazy Joe Devola is after Jerry[C20]. She is nervous about him going underwater when he goes scuba diving[C21]. She continuously wants him to apply to Bloomingdale's executive training program[C22], a position that would likely be less lucrative than comedy for Jerry, but would be a much more stable career choice.

Helen is similarly involved and worried about Jerry's love life. She thinks very highly of her son, frequently asking sincerely "how can anyone not like you [Jerry][C23]?" Helen is always preoccupied with food. She instantly wants to fix Kramer something to eat[C24], fervently pays for Jerry's meal when they eat out together and brings an entire suitcase of cereal to the court in "The Finale[C26]."

Eruv Tavshilin is the most "Jewish mother" of Jewish rituals. Normally, there is a rabbinic rule against preparing food for an upcoming Sabbath during a holiday. However, when the holiday is

THE (UNOFFICIAL) SEINFELD HAGGADAH

The Midrash, calls the Jews time in Egypt the *Kur Habarzel*, or the "iron furnace." Our time in Egypt was very destructive to our physical and spiritual well-being — a crucible, more or less. At the same time, it left us bare, and gave us the ability to be true to who we are as a people of God.

When we burn our chametz, we destroy the chametz completely. We are left with matzah, the humble and simple bread. During Pesach, the matzah represents what is true to our identity as a people. The matzah survives, even if it remains slightly burned on the outside.

בי בה דו דום דום, בום בדום בום בו, בה דו, בה דה דום דום, דום דדום דום דום דום דום. בדה דו דום דדום.

If the first day of Passover falls on Friday (or also on Thursday outside of Israel) the following is said before Passover begins over a cooked and baked (frequently matzah) item, which is then saved and eaten on Shabbat.

בָּרוּךְ אַתָּה ה'
אֱלֹהֵינוּ מֶלֶךְ הָעוֹלָם,
אֲשֶׁר קִדְּשָׁנוּ בְּמִצְוֹתָיו,
וְצִוָּנוּ עַל מִצְוַת עֵרוּב.

בי בה דו דום דום, בום בדום בום בו, בה דו, בה דה דום דום, דום דדום דום דום דום דום. בדה דו דום דדום.

on Friday, this practice is untenable from a practical perspective. How can one ensure a proper Sabbath when Friday is not available to prepare? The Eruv Tavshilin is a built in halakhic way the Rabbis dealt with this problem their laws were causing. It is based on the principle of "Ho'il", which literally means "maybe." When you start food preparation before the holiday, you can continue preparing on the holiday because you can rationalize that maybe, "ho'il," guests will come and will eat the food you've made. In that way, you are no longer only cooking for tomorrow, but for today, which you were always allowed to do. This only applies when it is actually reasonable that what you are preparing might be used or eaten by a visitor.

One could easily imagine Helen Seinfeld using this logic on the first day of Pesach, believing that she must be prepared for a guest, or Jerry, to come over for an unexpected visit. Helen clearly taught the immense value of hospitality to Jerry. Kramer inevitably will stop by Jerry's apartment to grab something to eat. George and Elaine do the same as well, albeit not as constantly. Elaine, whom Jerry derides for popping in, may well show up even without calling. If there is someone who can faithfully say "guests might come," it's Jerry.

Jerry clearly learns hospitality from his mother, especially when it comes to Kramer, George and Elaine. In the episode "The Betrayal[C27]," we see a flashback to when Jerry moves into his apartment and has the following exchange with Kramer:

> KRAMER: Uh, you need any help, or..?
> JERRY: No, thanks. But I ordered a pizza. You want some of it?
> KRAMER: Uh, no, no, no. I couldn't impose.
> JERRY: Why not? We're neighbors. What's mine is yours.
> KRAMER: (Eyeing Jerry's empty apartment) Really?

Jerry instinctively invites others in, exhibiting his mother's trait of hospitality. We begin Maggid with Ha Lachma Anya which focuses on demonstrating that we care about hospitality. We invite guests into our home, demonstrating, at least for the moment, that we have Jerry's level of hospitality (though perhaps not quite at the level that Kramer enjoys).

The Late Dinner

In "The Suicide[C28]," Elaine has to fast for three days because of problems with an ulcer. Elaine asks Jerry "Hey, have you ever fasted?" To which Jerry replies "Well, once I didn't have dinner until, like 9:00 o'clock, that was pretty rough." I wonder what Jerry would have said about a summer Friday night sing-along Kabbalat Shabbat.

The rabbis in the Talmud expect everyone to come to the Seder hungry — hungry like Jerry "kinda was that one time." According to Jewish law, one is not supposed to eat food of any kind after Mincha (the afternoon prayer) time, about three hours before the holiday starts. We are supposed to arrive at the Seder with hearty appetites so we can enjoy the night's iconic (albeit difficult to digest) dishes like matzah and Hillel's Sandwich. We are similarly supposed to arrive at Pesach with an appetite for the matzah. Many have the custom to refrain from eating matzah during the 30 days before Pesach.

One can have an early dinner before the Seder, but it must commence before 4:30 PM[C29], similar to the custom of the retirement community of Del Boca Vista. (This timing is especially fortuitous if that's when the dinner prices are cheapest.) And anyways, because chametz is already not permitted five hours earlier, you can't start

THE (UNOFFICIAL) SEINFELD HAGGADAH

Put the Seder plate on the table with a shankbone, roasted egg, horseradish, romaine lettuce, a vegetable, and haroset (a compound of nuts, fruits, and wine). Also, place a plate with three matzot and a bowl of salt water near the Seder plate.

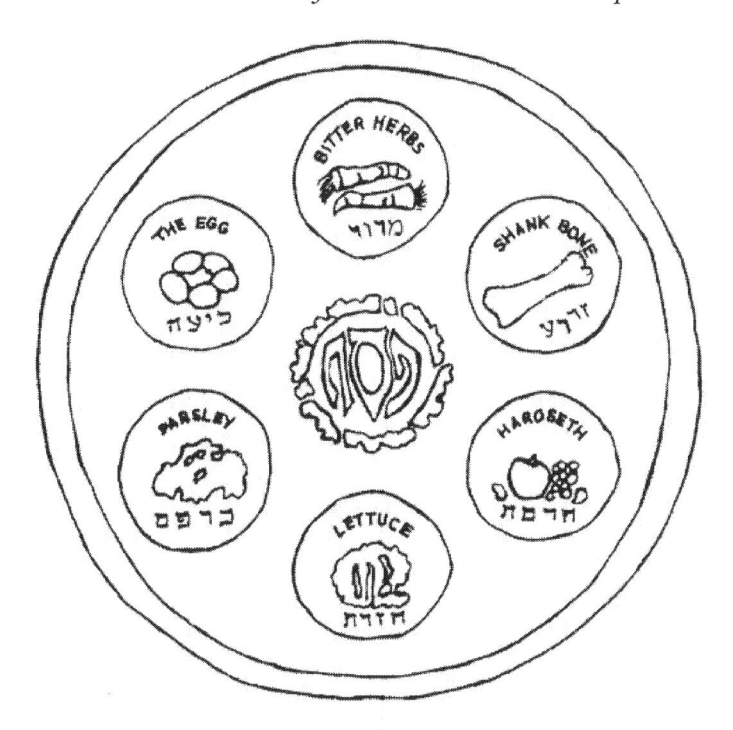

בי בה דו דום דום, בום בדום בום בו, בה דו, בה דה דום דום, דום דדום דום דום דום דום. בדה דו דום דדום.

your "fast" the way Jerry says Gandhi did: "I heard he used to polish off a box of Triscuits[C30]."

The Even Stevens Plate

In the show, Jerry is a very even-keeled character. Reviewers frequently consider him the comedic "straight man," against whom the other characters play. This equanimity is telegraphed by Jerry's nonchalant attitude, exemplified by his common adage "that's a shame," which he drops into conversations in an unconcerned manner when something horrible occurs.

In "The Serenity Now[C31]," Jerry's attitude is particularly noticed by his girlfriend Patty, who wants to see Jerry get mad. Jerry argues that he gets "peeved," "miffed," and "irked," but Patty wants to see him get really mad. Patty's observation that Jerry never shows his feelings is largely true; Jerry is not an emotional character. This status quo is what makes it particularly (and hilariously) jarring when the

הכנות — 13

floodgates of his emotions are let out. At one point he begins to cry and he is so unaccustomed to crying that he asks "What is this salty discharge?"

Similarly, in "The Opposite[C32]," Jerry realizes that not only is his personality even-keeled, his life is too. When he loses a gig, he gets a new one. He always evens out in poker and always has one friend doing well, and one who is not (usually George). Kramer gives him the fitting nickname "Even Stevens."

The symbols on Pesach are all very "Even Stevens." They represent freedom while simultaneously evoking slavery and tragedy. Think about matzah. Matzah is first talked about in the Haggadah as "Lechem Oni," the poor man's bread. It is the bread our poor enslaved ancestors ate in Egypt. At the same time, the poor man's bread is meant to symbolize freedom; it's the bread we quickly took as we were escaping Egypt. We are supposed to lean while eating our matzah, a gesture associated with royalty, even though we are eating "Lechem Oni."

All the items on the Seder plate share a similar dialectical nature. The bitter herbs, which customarily take up two spots on the Seder plate, represent both the bitterness of slavery and the mercy God showed us by taking us out of Egypt. Horseradish, the vile weed[C33], with its sharp taste, represents the pain of slavery. The second bitter herb, usually understood as romaine lettuce or "chazeret" (Hebrew)"chasa"(Aramaic), has a bitter aftertaste even if it's not nearly as bitter as horseradish. The Aramaic word for romaine, chasa, comes from the word "mercy." Even maror, the panultimate symbol of slavery, is a symbol of God's mercy and our ultimate freedom from the pain of Egypt.

Charoset, a sweet dish usually made of apples, walnuts, and sweet

═ BEE BA DO DUM DUM, BUM BADUM BUM BUH, BAH DUH, BAH DAH DUM DUM, DUM DEDUM DUM DUM DUM DUM. BADA DO DUM DEDUM. ═

The candles are lit, and we say the following blessings: [On Shabbat, add parts in brackets]

Blessed are You, Lord our God, King of the universe, who made us holy with His commandments, and commanded us to kindle the flame of [the Sabbath and] the festival.

Blessed are You, Lord our God, King of the universe, who has granted us life and sustenance and permitted us to reach this season.

wine, is also "Even Stevens" in nature. The Talmud (Pesachim 114a) discusses that the charoset is meant to counteract the bitterness of the maror. At the same time, Rambam and others understand the charoset to represent the mortar of the bricks our ancestors used to build the Egyptian cities while enslaved. Charoset simultaneously eases the burden of our pain, while reminding us of our backbreaking labor. The egg on the Seder plate represents both joy and mourning. It stands in for the Chagigah sacrifice, the special sacrifice given on all Festivals. Rema, an influential decisor from 16th century Poland, discusses how the egg is also supposed to be a food of mourning by reminding us that we cannot eat the actual Pascal sacrifice in the Temple. Many eat an egg dipped in saltwater at the beginning of the meal to heighten the sorrowful symbolism.

Karpas, the vegetable on the plate, is dialectical as well. It reminds us of spring — Pesach itself is sometimes known as Chag Haaviv (the spring holiday). It is also eaten dipped in salt water to represent the tears of our enslaved ancestors.

The shankbone (zeroa) is supposed to remind us of the Paschal sacrifice and the "strong arm" with which God took us out of Egypt. However, we do not eat the shankbone because while it represents the Paschal sacrifice, it is not supposed to be mistaken for the sacrifice itself. It both reminds us of our customs when the Temple stood, and that the Temple is no longer.

Through the Seder plate's rich symbolism, we present a nuanced approach to our history. Everything is a mixture of good and bad, of slavery and freedom. Let us think like Jerry towards our history, understanding that life has ups and downs. Like Jerry, we should never be too despondent nor too elated. The Seder plate entreats us to always be "Even Stevens."

בי בה דו דום דום, בום בדום בום בו, בה דו, בה דה דום דום, דום דדום דום דום דום, בדה דו דום דדום.

The candles are lit, and we say the following blessings: [On Shabbat, add parts in brackets]

בָּרוּךְ אַתָּה ה' אֱלֹהֵינוּ מֶלֶךְ הָעוֹלָם, אֲשֶׁר קִדְּשָׁנוּ בְּמִצְוֹתָיו, וְצִוָּנוּ לְהַדְלִיק נֵר שֶׁל [שַׁבָּת וְ]יוֹם טוֹב.

בָּרוּךְ אַתָּה ה' אֱלֹהֵינוּ מֶלֶךְ הָעוֹלָם, שֶׁהֶחֱיָנוּ וְקִיְּמָנוּ וְהִגִּיעָנוּ לַזְּמַן הַזֶּה.

Order of the Seder

Kadesh Urchatz. Karpas Yachatz. Maggid Rachtzah. Motzi Matzah. Maror Korech. Shulchan Orech. Tzafun Barech. Hallel Nirtzah.

<small>BEE BA DO DUM DUM, BUM BADUM BUM BUH, BAH DUH, BAH DAH DUM DUM, DUM DEDUM DUM DUM DUM DUM. BADA DO DUM DEDUM.</small>

The Seder Nazi

Seinfeld is much more scripted than people realize. While the characters might seem to be ad libbing at times, the dialogue was carefully written and delivered to the actors. Larry David was known to be draconian about the storyline's script, down to the exact wording of the jokes. This is in clear distinction from David's more recent show *Curb Your Enthusiasm*, which was scripted but allowed the actors a lot of creative license. *Seinfeld*'s rigidly scripted nature brings to mind one of the show's most iconic side characters: Yev Kassem, AKA the "Soup Nazi." In "The Soup Nazi[C34]," Yev makes unbelievably excellent soup — soup so good Jerry breaks up with his girlfriend to have some. However, Yev is called the "Soup Nazi" because he is very particular with the ordering procedure. Customers who deviate are denied soup — told, "NO SOUP FOR YOU!" — and must leave the store without a bowl. Customers who dare to purposely disrespect the rules are banned from the store for a year, or, in the case of Elaine, forever.

The Seder itself is tightly scripted as well. The Haggadah in front of you has virtually the same text as everyone else's (at least the Hebrew). We are instructed what to say, when to say it, and how to act when we are saying it. The name "Seder," literally means order. There is a specific structure to the night. We begin the Seder by singing the order, establishing the evening's framework to be sure we stick to it.

At the same time, no two Seders are the same. The outcome of a Seder is inextricably linked to the personalities in attendance and the wisdom, humor, and food they all share. The Seder's structure provides us with a launching off point to discuss the Exodus story and what it means to be a member of the Jewish people. The order of the Seder is not where the Seder ends, but where it begins.

THE (UNOFFICIAL) SEINFELD HAGGADAH

סִימָנֵי הַסֵּדֶר

קַדֵּשׁ וּרְחַץ. כַּרְפַּס יַחַץ. מַגִּיד רַחְצָה. מוֹצִיא מַצָּה. מָרוֹר כּוֹרֵךְ. שֻׁלְחָן עוֹרֵךְ. צָפוּן בָּרֵךְ. הַלֵּל נִרְצָה.

בי בה דו דום דום, בום בדום בום בן, בה דו, בה דה דום דום, דום דדום דום דום דום דום. בדה דו דום דדום.

Prayer in Judaism is also this way. The word Siddur, or prayer book, comes from the same root as the Seder, meaning order. While we are provided a structure with which to pray, prayer is also called "Avodah ShebaLev," service of the heart. How the words are said and infused with personal intention and meaning truly defines our prayers.

The *Seinfeld* script is very similar. While the jokes and script are first class, it is actually not the script that Larry David believes was the best part of the show. In an interview with "60 Minutes," he responded to a question about why the show was so successful with the following: "It's the actors. Because they're great actors. This material in the hands of other actors would be a disaster." Like a Seder, *Seinfeld* was scripted, but the people involved defined it.

In the same episode of "60 Minutes," Jerry took this idea one step further. In describing how they were able to discuss taboo topics, he remarked: "That's part of the game. It's like playing by the rules. That's what makes the game fun, without the rules it's not fun." Having a framework actually allows for creativity to flow. When anything is possible, it can be hard to figure out what to do. Having rules, whether in comedy or Pesach or prayer, can allow inspiration and opportunity to grow.

Neglecting these lessons was Yev Kassem's downfall. His harsh reaction to Elaine ends up costing him dearly — when she finds his recipes, she exacts revenge and publishes them. With the secret of his recipes available to all, his power is gone. For Yev, it is not *how* he makes his soup but the combination of the ingredients that is special. He does not understand that soup making is more than a science but an art. Perhaps had he internalized this, he could have survived the recipes' publication. May your Seder have more than the 15 ingredients you are about to sing, and may the structure provided invite the type of success that the *Seinfeld* actors were able to achieve.

THE HAGGADAH ABOUT NOTHING

Kadesh

We pour the first cup of wine (can you smell the first cup? Probably, because it isn't Hennigan's[1]). The matzot are covered.

> *On Shabbat, begin here:*
> And there was night (guy) and there was morning (guy[2]), the sixth day. And the heaven and the earth were finished, and all their host. And on the seventh day, God finished His work which He had done; and He rested on the seventh day from all His work which He had done. And God blessed the seventh day, and sanctified it, because on it He rested from all of His work which God had created and done. And Mr. Kruger didn't notice at all because he doesn't care, and it shows[3] (Genesis 1:31-2:3, kinda).

═ BEE BA DO DUM DUM, BUM BADUM BUM BUH, BAH DUH, BAH DAH DUM DUM, DUM DEDUM DUM DUM DUM DUM. BADA DO DUM DEDUM. ═

The Kadesh Control

The main characters in Seinfeld are obsessed with controlling their surroundings. George, in particular, has a pronounced need to control almost any situation. In "The Non-Fat Yogurt[C35]," George gets caught nudging Jerry to make fun of his nemesis Lloyd Braun. To control the situation, George pretends to have a disorder that causes his arm to move involuntarily. He tries to control the narrative to such an extent that he even goes to the doctor's appointment that Llyod Braun sets up for him, playing dangerously into the fiction just to keep up the veneer. George has no qualms about faking a real illness, telling Jerry: "I don't care. Look, Lloyd doesn't know what he's up against. This is nothing to me. My whole life is a lie." In order to exert control over his surroundings, George believes almost any lie is worth it. The situation ends poorly when George starts to fear that the twitch he had been faking is now real. Ironically, it is George's need for control that causes him to lose control of his arm.

Similarly, in "The Calzones[C36]," George tries to control his relationship with Mr. Steinbrenner by hooking him on calzones. In "The Comeback[C37]," George's desire to control conversations becomes apparent when he spends the entire episode trying to recreate a

THE (UNOFFICIAL) SEINFELD HAGGADAH

קַדֵּשׁ

We pour the first cup of wine (can you smell the first cup? Probably, because it isn't Hennigan's). The matzot are covered.

On Shabbat, begin here:

וַיְהִי עֶרֶב וַיְהִי בֹקֶר יוֹם הַשִּׁשִּׁי. וַיְכֻלּוּ הַשָּׁמַיִם וְהָאָרֶץ וְכָל־צְבָאָם. וַיְכַל אֱלֹהִים בַּיּוֹם הַשְּׁבִיעִי מְלַאכְתּוֹ אֲשֶׁר עָשָׂה וַיִּשְׁבֹּת בַּיּוֹם הַשְּׁבִיעִי מִכָּל מְלַאכְתּוֹ אֲשֶׁר עָשָׂה. וַיְבָרֶךְ אֱלֹהִים אֶת יוֹם הַשְּׁבִיעִי וַיְקַדֵּשׁ אֹתוֹ כִּי בוֹ שָׁבַת מִכָּל־מְלַאכְתּוֹ אֲשֶׁר בָּרָא אֱלֹהִים לַעֲשׂוֹת. (בראשית א, לא - ב, ג)

בי בה דו דום דום, בום בדום בום בו, בה דו, בה דה דום דום, דום דדום דום דום דום. בדה דו דום דום.

---

scenario so he can use the perfect comeback to a joke that was made at his expense. In "The Rye[C38]," George has Jerry send a marble rye up to his girlfriend's apartment with a fishing rod to convince her parents (the Rosses) his parents did not take back the rye when it wasn't served at their dinner together.

While George focuses on lowly matters and tries to control them, Kadesh has a loftier goal. We take wine, so easily used for drunkenness, and consecrate it, elevating it to holiness. We express our freedom by asserting control over our surroundings, even with items like wine which is inherently more difficult to control. Rabbi Yosef Tzvi Rimon, a major Israeli halakhic decissor, educator and author, observes that this step is called Kadesh and not Kiddush, like this prayer is on Shabbat. While Kiddush is a noun, referring to the blessing we recite, Kadesh is a verb, the action of creating the holiness of the Festivals. The dates of Festivals are defined by when we actively sanctify the months (even if they are now scheduled), but Shabbat comes every sunset on Friday no matter what. On Pesach, the first of the Festivals, we symbolize our freedom by controlling

קדש — 19

THE HAGGADAH ABOUT NOTHING

On weekdays, begin here: [On Shabbat, add parts in brackets]

Blessed are You, Lord our God, King of the universe, who creates the (mackinaw[4]) fruit of the vine.

Blessed are You, Lord our God, King of the universe, who has chosen us from all peoples and has raised us above all tongues and has sanctified us with His commandments. And You have given us, Lord our God, with love [Sabbaths for rest], appointed times for happiness, holidays and special times for joy, [this Sabbath day, and] this Festivus[5] of Matzot, our season of Freedom (our summer of George[6]) [in love] a sacred gathering in memory of the Exodus from Egypt. For You have chosen us and sanctified us above all peoples. And have given us for our inheritance, Your [holy Sabbath, and] special times for happiness and joy. Blessed are You, O Lord, who sanctifies [the Sabbath,] Israel, and the Festivals.

On Saturday night, continue on the next page.
On all other nights, continue on page 24.

═ BEE BA DO DUM DUM, BUM BADUM BUM BUH, BAH DUH, BAH DAH DUM DUM, DUM DEDUM DUM DUM DUM DUM. BADA DO DUM DEDUM. ═

time and do so by controlling a substance, wine, that is difficult to control.

In contradistinction to our efforts to uplift wine, in all the examples above, George brings everyone down to a more mundane level. Not only is he forced to continue lying to Llyod, but George, alongside Jerry, is forced to continue lying to his family and friends. Instead of using the calzones, and Steinbrenner's fascination for them, to do good for the organization, he uses it as a power grab to further his own interests. George is so persistent with the rye bread that Jerry feels the need to steal the last loaf, and George gets caught by the Rosses. Had George tried to control his situations in a less mundane way, in the way Kadesh asks us to, perhaps he would not be so tortured.

The Better Bubbly

On Pesach night, there is a specific requirement to use wine for the four cups. The Rabbis in the Talmud (Pesachim 108b) stated

20 — KADESH

THE (UNOFFICIAL) SEINFELD HAGGADAH

On weekdays, begin here: [On Shabbat, add parts in brackets]

סָבְרִי מָרָנָן וְרַבָּנָן וְרַבּוֹתַי:
בָּרוּךְ אַתָּה ה', אֱלֹהֵינוּ מֶלֶךְ הָעוֹלָם בּוֹרֵא פְּרִי הַגָּפֶן.
בָּרוּךְ אַתָּה ה', אֱלֹהֵינוּ מֶלֶךְ הָעוֹלָם, אֲשֶׁר בָּחַר בָּנוּ מִכָּל-עָם וְרוֹמְמָנוּ מִכָּל-לָשׁוֹן וְקִדְּשָׁנוּ בְּמִצְוֹתָיו. וַתִּתֶּן לָנוּ ה' אֱלֹהֵינוּ בְּאַהֲבָה [שַׁבָּתוֹת לִמְנוּחָה וּ]מוֹעֲדִים לְשִׂמְחָה, חַגִּים וּזְמַנִּים לְשָׂשׂוֹן, [אֶת יוֹם הַשַׁבָּת הַזֶּה וְ]אֶת יוֹם חַג הַמַּצּוֹת הַזֶּה זְמַן חֵרוּתֵנוּ, [בְּאַהֲבָה] מִקְרָא קֹדֶשׁ זֵכֶר לִיצִיאַת מִצְרָיִם. כִּי בָנוּ בָחַרְתָּ וְאוֹתָנוּ קִדַּשְׁתָּ מִכָּל הָעַמִּים, [וְשַׁבָּת] וּמוֹעֲדֵי קָדְשֶׁךָ [בְּאַהֲבָה וּבְרָצוֹן]

בְּשִׂמְחָה וּבְשָׂשׂוֹן הִנְחַלְתָּנוּ. בָּרוּךְ אַתָּה ה', מְקַדֵּשׁ [הַשַׁבָּת וְ]יִשְׂרָאֵל וְהַזְּמַנִּים.

On Saturday night, continue on the next page.
On all other nights, continue on page 25

that in order to fulfill the obligation to drink the four cups, one must dilute the wine. (In the days when the Seder was created, wine was very concentrated. Drinking it undiluted would get the person intoxicated quickly.) At the Seder, wine is supposed to be high class and enjoyable, rather than a quick way to get drunk.

This is what George misunderstands during "The Dinner Party[C39]" when he and Elaine have the following conversation:

GEORGE: I don't even drink wine. I drink Pepsi.
ELAINE: You can't bring Pepsi.
GEORGE: Why not?
ELAINE: Because we're adults?
GEORGE: You telling me that wine is better than Pepsi? Huh, no way wine is better than Pepsi.
JERRY: I'm telling you George, I don't think we want to walk in there and put a big plastic jug of Pepsi on the table.

קדש — 21

On Saturday night, add the following paragraph:

Blessed are You, Lord our God, King of the universe, who creates the light of the fire. Blessed are You, Lord our God, King of the universe, who distinguishes between the holy and the mundane, between the light and the (Other Side of) Darkness[7], between Israel and the nations, between the seventh day and the six working days. You have distinguished between the holiness of the Sabbath and the holiness of the Festivals, and You have sanctified the seventh day above the six working days. You have distinguished and sanctified Your people Israel with Your holiness. Blessed are You, O Lord, who distinguishes between the holy and the holy.

BEE BA DO DUM DUM, BUM BADUM BUM BUH, BAH DUH, BAH DAH DUM DUM, DUM DEDUM DUM DUM DUM DUM. BADA DO DUM DEDUM.

George believes that since he enjoys Pepsi more than wine, it is appropriate to bring Pepsi to a dinner party rather than wine. He envisions that people will come up to him and say, "Just between you and me, I'm really excited about the Ring Dings and the Pepsi. Europeans with the Beaujolais and Chardonnay..."

If George were to attend a Seder his thinking is mistaken. The reason we drink wine at the Seder is not because it is necessarily our favorite drink, but because it is the drink of free people who are "adults." We drink the four cups to remember the four expressions of redemption used in Exodus 6:6-7: "I [God] will rescue you, save you, redeem you, and take you out." We are trying to create an atmosphere of freedom, class, and sophistication that Elaine and Jerry clearly understand. One wonders how George would perform at his first Seder. Hopefully, better than a Festivus meal at his parent's house.

Oh, and Pepsi wasn't Kosher for Pesach back then.

The Reclining

The Sages decreed that one must recline while drinking the four cups of wine and eating the matzah at the Seder. We are supposed to appear as though we personally were freed from the bondage of Egypt.

Multiple times throughout Seinfeld, George's preoccupation with being comfortable gets him in trouble. In "The Reverse Peephole[C40]," the gang decides to buy Joe Mayo, a mutual friend, a massage chair as an apartment gift. Although they split the cost four ways, a

THE (UNOFFICIAL) SEINFELD HAGGADAH

On Saturday night, add the following paragraph:

בָּרוּךְ אַתָּה ה', אֱלֹהֵינוּ מֶלֶךְ הָעוֹלָם, בּוֹרֵא מְאוֹרֵי הָאֵשׁ. בָּרוּךְ אַתָּה ה', אֱלֹהֵינוּ מֶלֶךְ הָעוֹלָם הַמַּבְדִיל בֵּין קֹדֶשׁ לְחֹל, בֵּין אוֹר לְחֹשֶׁךְ, בֵּין יִשְׂרָאֵל לָעַמִּים, בֵּין יוֹם הַשְּׁבִיעִי לְשֵׁשֶׁת יְמֵי הַמַּעֲשֶׂה. בֵּין קְדֻשַּׁת שַׁבָּת לִקְדֻשַּׁת יוֹם טוֹב הִבְדַּלְתָּ, וְאֶת־יוֹם הַשְּׁבִיעִי מִשֵּׁשֶׁת יְמֵי הַמַּעֲשֶׂה קִדַּשְׁתָּ. הִבְדַּלְתָּ וְקִדַּשְׁתָּ אֶת־עַמְּךָ יִשְׂרָאֵל בִּקְדֻשָּׁתֶךָ. בָּרוּךְ אַתָּה ה', הַמַּבְדִיל בֵּין קֹדֶשׁ לְקֹדֶשׁ.

בִּי בָּה דוּ דוֹם דוֹם, בּוֹם בְּדוֹם בּוֹם בּוֹ, בָּה דוּ, בָּה דָה דוֹם דוֹם, דוֹם דְדוֹם דוֹם דוֹם דוֹם דוֹם. בָּדָה דוּ דוֹם דְדוֹם.

delivery mishap lands the chair in George's apartment. George ends up enjoying the chair so much that he ultimately pays for it himself after his friends pull out one by one, while George can't admit it was sent to him. In "The Nap[C41]," George decides to build a place to sleep in his office under his desk while working for the Yankees. He takes advantage of this until he gets caught by the Yankee's owner, Mr. Steinbrenner. When there is a fake bomb scare, Steinbrenner panics and runs to hide under George's desk, unaware of how George has repurposed the space. Though the episode ends before George is discovered, we are left to imagine the horror of being caught sleeping under your desk at work by the organization's owner. Similarly, when George receives a three month severance package after being fired from the Yankees, he declares the time the "summer of George." His first item on the agenda: "I bought a recliner with a fridge built right into it." (Needless to say, the "summer of George" is not very productive.)

קדש — 23

THE HAGGADAH ABOUT NOTHING

On all days, continue here:

Blessed are You, Lord our God, King of the universe, who has granted us life and sustenance and permitted us to reach this season.

Drink the majority of the cup while reclining to the left.

BEE BA DO DUM DUM, BUM BADUM BUM BUH, BAH DUH, BAH DAH DUM DUM, DUM DEDUM DUM DUM DUM DUM. BADA DO DUM DEDUM.

In all three cases, George understands sleeping and reclining as a way of abrogating responsibility and being free to waste his time as he wishes. But is this all there is to reclining or is there something more?

The answer may be found in Jerry's standup at the beginning of "The Finale[C42]":

> JERRY: It seems like whenever these office people call you in for a meeting, the whole thing is about the sitting down. I would really like to sit down with you. I think we need to sit down and talk. Why don't you come in, and we'll sit down. Well, sometimes the sitting down doesn't work. People get mad at the sitting. You know, we've been sitting here for I don't know how long. How much longer are we just going to sit here? I'll tell you what I think we should do. I think we should all sleep on it. Maybe we're not getting down low enough. Maybe if we all lie down, then our brains will work.

When you are in a more relaxed position, you are more open

24 — KADESH

THE (UNOFFICIAL) SEINFELD HAGGADAH

On all days, continue here:

בָּרוּךְ אַתָּה ה' אֱלֹהֵינוּ מֶלֶךְ הָעוֹלָם, שֶׁהֶחֱיָנוּ וְקִיְּמָנוּ וְהִגִּיעָנוּ לַזְּמַן הַזֶּה.

Drink the majority of the cup while reclining to the left.

בִּי בַּה דוּ דוּם דוּם, בּוּם בְּדוּם בּוּם בּוֹ, בַּה דוּ, בַּה דַה דוּם דוּם, דוּם דְדוּם דוּם דוּם דוּם דוּם. בְּדַה דוּ דוּם דוּם.

to ideas. By physically unburdening yourself, you are able to engage with your surroundings in a different way. Reclining is an action where you create the environment necessary to think freely, and not a passive liberation from responsibility. When we recline at the Seder, we not only feel like free people, and more predisposed to act and think like liberated people as well.

By reclining, we can act like we are the head of the Ottomon Empire: "a whole empire based on putting your feet up[C43]."

The Special Fruit

We recite the Shehecheyanu blessing when we realize the miracle of the moment we are in. This happens when we experience something new or novel, like eating a new fruit, wearing a newly tailored outfit, or on the special occasions of the Jewish Festivals. We say the Shehechiyanu blessing to start all Festivals, thanking God for bringing us to this specific moment.

In "The Doodle[C44]," Kramer becomes obsessed with a new fruit — namely, the Mackinaw peaches that ripen once a year and are "like a circus in your mouth." The day the peach ripens, he unknowingly spends ninety minutes in Jerry's apartment which was recently fumigated by an exterminator. Kramer loses his sense of taste and is distraught that he is missing out on the peaches that are only available for a short amount of time. While Newman hoards the peaches and devours them one by one, Kramer can't enjoy them at all. By the end of the episode when Kramer finally recovers his taste, he sees Newman savoring the last Mackinaw peach (Newman heartlessly offers him to "suck the pit" with a maniacal laugh). We are left to imagine how much Kramer would have enjoyed it. It is the feeling of tasting the "miracle of nature that exists for a brief moment in time" that is embodied by the Mackinaw peach that we invoke when we say Shehecheyanu blessing.

קדש — 25

THE HAGGADAH ABOUT NOTHING

And Wash

Wash your hands but do not say the blessing "on the washing of the hands." Especially true for the person who prepared the Karpas because how would one explain not eating the Karpas?[8]

═══ BEE BA DO DUM DUM, BUM BADUM BUM BUH, BAH DUH, BAH DAH DUM DUM, DUM DEDUM DUM DUM DUM DUM. BADA DO DUM DEDUM. ═══

The Hand Washing

Handwashing as a practice and concept recurs throughout the *Seinfeld* series. In "The Voice[C45]," Kramer's intern, Darren, who works for his "company" Kramerica Industries, is tasked with going to lunch with Jerry and George and taking notes so Kramer can be filled in about what happened. When Jerry goes to the bathroom, Darren reports: "Then Mr. Seinfeld went to the restroom, at which point Mr. Costanza scooped ice out of Mr. Seinfeld's drink with his bare hands using it to wash up, then Mr. Costanza remarked to me, 'This never happened.'" (Jerry then spits out the water, while George looks embarrassed.) Similarly, in "The Pie[C46]," Jerry is in the bathroom at Poppies restaurant when Poppie himself, who happens to be the father of Jerry's then-girlfriend, leaves the bathroom without washing his hands. Jerry can't explain to his girlfriend that her father doesn't wash his hands, so he just refuses without explanation when served his food. His girlfriend misinterprets his actions as retaliation for her not explaining why she wouldn't take a bite out of his apple pie at Monk's earlier that day. The storyline has a payoff when Jerry is at the restaurant when Poppies gets shut down for health code violations, as Jerry says: "Well, Poppie's a little sloppy." In the Seder, handwashing has a different and higher purpose than hygiene (or lack thereof).

At the Seder, we are not only trying to recreate the Pesach story but also the traditional eating of the Temple-period Paschal sacrifice. We eat together as a group as we did then, and many men have the custom to wear their white kittels, a traditional garment

THE (UNOFFICIAL) SEINFELD HAGGADAH

וּרְחַץ

Wash your hands but do not say the blessing "on the washing of the hands." Especially true for the person who prepared the Karpas because how would one explain not eating the Karpas?

בִּי בַּה דוּ דוּ דוֹם דוֹם, בּוֹם בַּדוֹם בּוֹם בּוֹ, בַּה דוּ, בַּה דַה דוֹם דוֹם, דוֹם דַדוֹם דוֹם דוֹם דוֹם דוֹם. בַּדַה דוּ דוֹם דַדוֹם.

resembling the priestly garments of the high priests, who performed the sacrifice. Additionally, before eating any food that is wet, our ancestors would wash their hands because wet foods are subject to ritual defilement.

Since we are about to eat the Karpas dipped in salt water at this point in the Seder, we try to recreate what we would have done during Temple times. In doing so, handwashing becomes not only a cleanliness activity but one that connects us to the Pesachs of yore. Through this ritual we bind ourselves to our history and what it means to be part of the Jewish people. Simultaneously, we pray for a future with a Temple where we will once again need to wash before eating wet vegetables.

Then again, if, like Kramer, you live in the shower, you can wash and wet your vegetables at the same time (which is convenient if you're not a germaphobe[C47].)

Greens

Take from the greens; dip it, as Joe Dimaggio does with his dinky donuts[9], into the salt water; say the blessing below, and have in mind that this blessing will also be for the bitter herbs. Eat without reclining.

Blessed are you, Lord our God, King of the universe, who creates the produce of the soil.

═ BEE BA DO DUM DUM, BUM BADUM BUM BUH, BAH DUH, BAH DAH DUM DUM, DUM DEDUM DUM DUM DUM DUM. BADA DO DUM DEDUM. ═

The Fancy Appetizer

In "The Pledge Drive[C48]," Elaine notices that her boss Mr. Pitt eats his (Ashkenazi kitniyot warning) Snickers candy bar with a fork and a knife. While Elaine and Jerry are confused by this, George is not. Thinking the behavior high class, George does the same during a work meeting at the Yankees office. When asked why he is using a fork and knife to cut a Snickers bar he answers: "I am eating my dessert, how do you eat it, with your hands?" George turns out to be right. Not only is he listened to for "trying to have the Yankees reach another strata of society," his coworkers begin to eat their desserts with utensils as well. This begins a trend spreading all the way back to Monk's coffee shop, where Elaine and Jerry see everyone following suit.

One way people attain higher status is by imitating those that are already the elites. Frequently, this is done with food. The Snickers bar is a good example, but Karpas is too. The Bach, a prominent 16th-17th century Eastern European Halakhist, states that we purposely treat the Seder the way the Roman elites would treat their important dinners. They would serve hors d'oeuvres, followed by the program, and ending with dinner. As free people, we treat our Seder the way important people treat their dinners.

This custom is still alive and well at Jewish weddings, where the festivities begin with hors d'oeuvres or a shmorg, followed by the ceremony, followed by the meal. The karpas is part of treating our Seder as we would a wedding or other important ceremony. We begin the food of our Seder with Karpas as if we are eating a Snickers with a fork and knife. We act like Mr. Pitt "classing up the place."

THE (UNOFFICIAL) SEINFELD HAGGADAH

כַּרְפַּס

Take from the greens; dip it, as Joe Dimaggio does with his dinky donuts, into the salt water; say the blessing below, and have in mind that this blessing will also be for the bitter herbs. Eat without reclining.

בָּרוּךְ אַתָּה ה' אֱלֹהֵינוּ מֶלֶךְ הָעוֹלָם, בּוֹרֵא פְּרִי הָאֲדָמָה.

THE HAGGADAH ABOUT NOTHING

Break

Split the middle matzah in two, and conceal the larger piece in a case to use it for the afikoman, because important things go in a case[10].

BEE BA DO DUM DUM, BUM BADUM BUM BUH, BAH DUH, BAH DAH DUM DUM, DUM DEDUM DUM DUM DUM DUM. BADA DO DUM DEDUM.

The Matza Breaking

Why do we break the matzah at the Seder? The Gemara (Brachot 39b) discusses how it is necessary to have a broken piece to memorialize the matzah as the bread of affliction, the poor man's bread. There is an argument over when to break the matzah — either directly before eating it (Rambam) or before Maggid (Rashi) which is our custom. Either way, the question remains: why do we break the matzah publicly at the Seder at all? There is certainly no shortage of broken pieces in the box.

An answer may be found based on the writings of the Netziv, the 19th century Russian Rosh Yeshiva and prolific writer (Shut Meishiv Davar (no. 21)). He writes that the meaning of a broken piece is relative. The matza is only considered truly broken if we see it break. We require empirical evidence to determine brokenness.

In *Seinfeld*, the characters assume the brokenness of others and judge people all the time. Elaine judges George for getting engaged and talks about him behind his back[C49]; Jerry, Elaine and Kramer judge George for getting a toupee (Elaine even throws it out of the window exclaiming, "I don't like this thing, and this is what I'm doing with it!"[C50]). The four main characters judge people for dating in public, and for saying "Happy New Year!" too late into the new year[C51].

In certain situations, this tendency gets them in trouble. In "The English Patient[C52]," Elaine is judged for not liking the movie "The English Patient," winner of nine (real life) academy awards. Her dislike of the popular movie causes all sorts of issues, including losing her boyfriend and almost getting fired. In "The Lip Reader[C53]," George has Jerry's girlfriend who can read lips help him spy on two coworkers. George judges his coworkers instantly when the lip reader misreads their conversation and misunderstands one of them saying "sweeping together." In that same episode, Jerry judges the lines woman at the US Open for not listening to him, when she is actually

THE (UNOFFICIAL) SEINFELD HAGGADAH

יַחַץ

Split the middle matzah in two, and conceal the larger piece in a case to use it for the afikoman, because important things go in a case.

בי בה דו דום דום, בום בדום בום בו, בה דו, בה דה דום דום, דום דדום דום דום דום דום. בדה דו דום דדום.

deaf. In "The Sniffling Accountant[C54]," Jerry and Kramer assume their accountant is on drugs because he is sniffing a lot. They end up losing money (for reasons too complicated to explain here) despite the fact he was just allergic to Jerry's mohair sweater. In "The Pony Remark[C55]," Jerry judges people who own ponies, saying that he "hates anyone who had a pony growing up." The comment upends a family dinner party when the elderly Manya says she had a pony in Poland. Consistently, the gang judges others for being "broken" without questioning their assumptions. We break the matzah publically in order to remind ourselves not to judge people unfavorably unless we fully understand the situation, because something is not broken unless we saw it break.

In "The Cadillac[C56]," we do see one moment of introspection. After the cable company makes Kramer wait for hours, Kramer continually makes Nick, the cable guy, wait to turn off extra channels Kramer accidentally had. Eventually the cable guy breaks down and goes on a monologue:

> NICK: (weary) Alright, I know you're in there. I know you can hear me. You win, okay? You win. I can't do it any more. What d'you want from me? Apology? Alright, I'm sorry. There, I said it, I'm sorry, I'm sorry. I see now how we made you feel when we made you sit home waiting. I dunno why we do it. (upset) I guess maybe we just kind of enjoy taking advantage of

people. (reasonable) Well, that's gonna change. From now on, no more 'nine to twelve,' no more 'one to five.' We're gonna have appointments. Eleven o'clock is gonna mean eleven o'clock. And, if we can't make it, we're gonna call you, tell you why. (worked up) For God's sakes, if a doctor can do it, why can't we? (almost sobbing) Anyway, that's it.

The cable guy's true understanding of what Kramer went through

═ BEE BA DO DUM DUM, BUM BADUM BUM BUH, BAH DUH, BAH DAH DUM DUM, DUM DEDUM DUM DUM DUM DUM. BADA DO DUM DEDUM. ═

The Recitation of the Passover Story

Uncover the matzot, raise the Seder plate, and say out loud:

HA LACHMA ANYA

This is the bread of affliction that our ancestors ate in the land of Egypt. Anyone who is famished should come and eat, for we can spare a square[11], anyone who is in need should come and partake of the Paschal sacrifice, but please wear a nametag[12]. This year we are here, next year we will be in the land of Israel; this year we are slaves, next year we will be free people. This year we are in a non pony country, next year may we be in a country filled with ponies[13].

═ BEE BA DO DUM DUM, BUM BADUM BUM BUH, BAH DUH, BAH DAH DUM DUM, DUM DEDUM DUM DUM DUM DUM. BADA DO DUM DEDUM. ═

The Invitations

At the beginning of Maggid, the part of the Haggadah that details the Exodus story, we say, "Anyone who is famished should come and eat, anyone who is in need should come and partake of the Pesach sacrifice." Even when we are able to invite guests to the Seder, is anyone really accepting our offer? We are extending the invitation from within our own houses, many of which are outfitted with alarm systems to keep strangers out. The likelihood of someone suddenly entering our home once the Seder has already begun is slim to none.

Rather than literally inviting someone in, the open invitation we start Maggid with is a virtue signal defining our Seder. In his is shown to be the remedy. While Kramer's actions are not kind, Nick is finally put in Kramer's shoes and can now fully understand what it is like to wait. When Kramer sees the cable guy "broken" the same way he was, he opens the door and gives him a huge hug. Until we are able to have that moment of understanding that Nick has, we cannot label anyone as "broken."

מַגִּיד

Uncover the matzot, raise the Seder plate, and say out loud:

הא לחמא עניא

הָא לַחְמָא עַנְיָא דִּי אֲכָלוּ אַבְהָתָנָא בְּאַרְעָא דְמִצְרָיִם. כָּל דִּכְפִין יֵיתֵי וְיֵיכֹל, כָּל דִּצְרִיךְ יֵיתֵי וְיִפְסַח. הָשַׁתָּא הָכָא, לְשָׁנָה הַבָּאָה בְּאַרְעָא דְיִשְׂרָאֵל. הָשַׁתָּא עַבְדֵי, לְשָׁנָה הַבָּאָה בְּנֵי חוֹרִין.

Piskei Corona, a set of his Rabbinic judgements during the ongoing COVID-19 pandemic, Rav Hershel Shachter, Rosh Yeshiva at Yeshiva University's Rabbinical School, says you should continue to extend this invitation even when you know guests won't show up, in order to commemorate the times of the Temple when everyone would eat together. Similarly, the Kol Bo, a Middle Ages collection of Jewish laws and rituals, notes that the invitation is supposed to commemorate the expeditious exit from Egypt when everyone had to share with one another to survive. In both explanations, we begin Maggid with the clarification that we are all part of one singular Jewish nation.

The four main Seinfeld characters do not see the world in this way. Aside from Kramer, none of them really have friends outside the group. In "The Bizarro Jerry[C57]," Elaine actually tries to make a new group of friends that appear to be the bizzaro (they look similar and have similar roles in the group, but are "good") versions of Jerry, George, and Kramer, but she fails to fit into their nice and friendly group culture. In "The Pool Guy[C58]," Jerry states to the pool worker

═ BEE BA DO DUM DUM, BUM BADUM BUM BUH, BAH DUH, BAH DAH DUM DUM, DUM DEDUM DUM DUM DUM DUM. BADA DO DUM DEDUM. ═

Cover the matzot. We pour the second cup of wine.

FOUR QUESTIONS

What's the deal[14] with this night being different than all other nights?

What's the deal that on all other nights we eat chametz and matzah; this night, only matzah?

═ BEE BA DO DUM DUM, BUM BADUM BUM BUH, BAH DUH, BAH DAH DUM DUM, DUM DEDUM DUM DUM DUM DUM. BADA DO DUM DEDUM. ═

The "What's the Deal?"

Questioning is nothing new to Jews or to *Seinfeld*. The show, and Jerry's standup, frequently begin with the refrain, "What's the deal with...?" The question becomes so expected that in "The Bookstore[C59]," Kramer tries to imitate Jerry by mimicking the expression into a wooden spoon: "Now, what's the deal with politics?" Through questioning, Jerry examines minutia and trivial quarrels with George or Elaine ad nauseum.

Similarly, the Haggadah starts, and is required to start, with questioning. The need to question is seemingly a biblical commandment. Regarding the Exodus story, Deuteronomy 13:14 states, "When, in the future, your child asks you..." We take that literally, questions must be asked. The custom is to follow the verse and have the children ask, but even if you are doing the Seder alone, the four questions should still be asked.

Both *Seinfeld* and the Seder fall into Socrates' philosophy that who is trying to befriend him, "Look Ramon, you're a nice guy. But, I actually only have three friends. I really can't handle any more." We should not emulate this unwelcoming nature. Being open to others is a feature of Judaism, especially during a holiday that commemorates us being strangers in a strange land. We start our Seder by saying explicitly that we can handle more friends, we "invite" everyone in and establish that we are part of a community.

בי בה דו דום דום, בום בדום בום בו, בה דו, בה דה דום דום, דום דדום דום דום דום דום. בדה דו דום דדום.

Cover the matzot. We pour the second cup of wine.

מה נשתנה

מַה נִּשְׁתַּנָּה הַלַּיְלָה הַזֶּה מִכָּל הַלֵּילוֹת?

שֶׁבְּכָל הַלֵּילוֹת אָנוּ אוֹכְלִין חָמֵץ וּמַצָּה, הַלַּיְלָה הַזֶּה – כֻּלּוֹ מַצָּה.

בי בה דו דום דום, בום בדום בום בו, בה דו, בה דה דום דום, דום דדום דום דום דום דום. בדה דו דום דדום.

"an unexamined life is not worth living." Questioning is integral to each person and to society as a whole. In Apology 30e Socrates states:

> For if you put me to death, you will not easily find another, who, to use a rather absurd figure, attaches himself to the city as a gadfly to a horse, which, though large and well bred, is sluggish on account of his size and needs to be aroused by stinging. I think the god fastened me upon the city in some such capacity, and I go about arousing,

Socrates sees himself as the "fly" arousing the "horse" of society with questions. In many ways, Jerry occupies this role as well by observing things about society and interrogating them. However, his observations frequently trap him, and his friends, in the mundane instead of getting him to go above his everyday life. In "The Bizarro Jerry[C60]," Elaine notices this trap saying: "I can't spend the rest of my life coming into this stinking apartment every ten minutes to pore over the excruciating minutiae of every single daily event."

She spends hours at a time examining the banalities of daily life without seeking to rise above the minutia. However, there are certain moments in the series when the characters do seek a higher level of thought. Whenever Jerry and George go to the beach (in a variety of episodes), they have a revelation. They are still using their questioning, but these times they get outside of their banal lives. In "The Opposite[C61]," George achieves success by doing the opposite of his instincts because, he reasons, "if every instinct you have is wrong, then the opposite would have to be right." In this moment, George is questioning every decision he has ever made. Once George extracts himself from the box of his regular behavior patterns, he improves his relationships, his job and his overall lifestyle. Similarly, in "The Abstinence[C62]," George is able to act differently when he looks at life differently. When George's girlfriend gets mono, they can't engage in physical intimacy for six weeks. George, unburdened by his constant fixation on sex, is able to focus on the rest of his life and excels. When individuals (even George) can rise above the pedantry of everyday life, they become better people.

The Seder asks us to question but also to rise above the mundane. While the questions we ask at the Seder might themselves be mundane —why are we eating matzah? Why are we leaning? — the answers to these queries are not. The answers refer to what it means to be God's people, what it means to be free, and the symbolism of our actions on Seder night. When we question, we do so to break free in a practical but also a spiritual sense, like Jerry and George at the beach. Sometimes during the Seder, we do the opposite. We eat matzah instead of chametz, sit differently, and eat bitter foods. Like Geroge, we do the opposite to break free from our regular lives. Perhaps people buy new Haggadahs each year in order to look at the Seder with fresh eyes. We certainly try to introspect and reevaluate throughout the year, but never more than on Seder night.

The Newman Chametz

The Torah treats Egypt the way Jerry treats Newman. Not only do we remember the Egyptian slavery and the atrocities that occured, we treat Egypt as inherently negative. The Torah tells us not to return to Egypt (Dueteronomy 17:16). While the scope of the prohibition is unclear, Egypt is the only country treated this way by the Torah. Even things from Egypt are viewed negatively. The King of Israel is prohibited from acquiring too many horses, explicitly because horses come from Egypt (ibid). We are told not to act in the ways of Egypt (Leviticus 18:3) and are warned that, should we sin, we will be thrown back "to the depths of Egypt" (Deuteronomy 28:68).

Historically, leavened bread has roots in ancient Egypt. The first known time yeast was used for baking was in ancient Egypt. Archaeologists digging in Egyptian ruins found early grinding stones and baking chambers for yeast-raised bread, and date the ruins to over 4000 years ago. Before that, bread would be left to rise without chemical assistance (the natural leavening agent in wheat makes it rise somewhat). Bread that rises with the help of yeast has a uniquely Egyptian pedigree.

Jerry treats Newman with the same disdain, albeit for unclear reasons. In "The Big Salad[C63]," Jerry visits Newman and treats his apartment the way the Torah treats Egypt: with disdain. Jerry describes that "my skin is crawling just being inside your little rat's nest." Jerry is so invested in hating Newman that he is unable to date a woman Newman previously dated. In the same episode, Jerry describes Newman as a "mystery wrapped in a twinkie." When Elaine suggests that "perhaps there's more to Newman than meets the eye," Jerry answers adamantly, "no, there's less."

On Pesach, we show the same disdain for Egypt and for chametz by association. When we left Egypt, we left the land of risen dough. The Torah wants us to reject Egypt completely, so it completely negates chametz. When we actively don't eat chametz on Pesach, we aren't just eating matzah, we are fully leaving behind our enslaved selves and looking towards a better future. May Jerry be able to look towards a better future with anything involving Newman.

מגיד — 37

What's the deal that on all other nights we eat other vegetables; tonight only maror?

What's the deal that on all other nights, we don't dip our food, even one time, but tonight we double dip[15]?

What's the deal that on all other nights, we eat either sitting or reclining; tonight we all recline?

═══ BEE BA DO DUM DUM, BUM BADUM BUM BUH, BAH DUH, BAH DAH DUM DUM, DUM DEDUM DUM DUM DUM DUM. BADA DO DUM DEDUM. ═══

The Double Dipping

Dipping is an odd custom at the Seder. In fact, many authorities (Rashi, Rambam, Tur to name a few) assume that it is intentionally odd. In an effort to elicit questions, we do certain things at the Seder that are purposefully unusual — dipping twice is one of those things. But, with so many unusual actions at our disposal, why is dipping singled out?

The answer may be found in "The Implant[C64]." While at a funeral, George dips the same chip twice. Timmy, George's grieving girlfriend's brother, notices, and he and George have the following exchange:

> TIMMY: What are you doing?
> GEORGE: What?
> TIMMY: Did...did you just double-dip that chip?
> GEORGE: Excuse me?
> TIMMY: You double-dipped the chip!
> GEORGE: "Double-dipped"? What are you talking about?
> TIMMY: You dipped the chip. You took a bite. <points at the dip> And you dipped again.
> GEORGE: So...?
> TIMMY: That's like putting your whole mouth right in the dip! From now on, when you take a chip - just take one dip and end it!
> GEORGE: Well, I'm sorry, Timmy...but I don't dip that way. <takes a chip.>
> TIMMY: Oh, you don't, huh?
> GEORGE: No. <dips the chip> You dip the way you want to dip... <bites the chip> I'll dip the way I want to dip. <dips the chip again.>
> TIMMY: Gimme the chip! <Grabs George and the chip goes flying.> Gimme the chip!

שֶׁבְּכָל הַלֵּילוֹת אָנוּ אוֹכְלִין שְׁאָר יְרָקוֹת – הַלַּיְלָה הַזֶּה (כֻּלּוֹ) מָרוֹר.

שֶׁבְּכָל הַלֵּילוֹת אֵין אָנוּ מַטְבִּילִין אֲפִילוּ פַּעַם אֶחָת – הַלַּיְלָה הַזֶּה שְׁתֵּי פְעָמִים.

שֶׁבְּכָל הַלֵּילוֹת אָנוּ אוֹכְלִין בֵּין יוֹשְׁבִין וּבֵין מְסֻבִּין – הַלַּיְלָה הַזֶּה כֻּלָּנוּ מְסֻבִּין.

בִּי בָּה דוּ דוּם דוּם, בּוּם בְּדוּם בּוּם בּוּ, בָּה דוּ, בָּה דָּה דוּם דוּם, דוּם דְּדוּם דוּם דוּם דוּם. בַּדָה דוּ דוּם דְּדוּם.

    When you dip wantonly, you establish a freedom to do as you please. Even if Timmy is overreacting, George is acting inappropriately by failing to be considerate of others. A funeral is certainly not a time for George to act like he owns the dip. But the concept of dipping as a luxurious way of eating is still true. During the Seder, it is more than appropriate to act like royalty and dip. Dipping our food shows our ability to eat as we please. Still — maybe don't take a bite and then dip again, even at the Seder. Others are trying to act royally, too.

מגיד — 39

THE HAGGADAH ABOUT NOTHING

The matzot should stay untucked for the duration of maggid. Some matzot untucked and some tucked is acceptable as well, but it's easier if they are all untucked[16].

WE WERE SLAVES IN EGYPT

We were slaves to Pharaoh in the land of Egypt, but the Lord, our God, took us out from there with a strong (man[17]) hand and an outstretched forearm. Now, we're out there and we're loving every minute of it[18]. And if the Holy One, blessed be He, had not taken our ancestors from Egypt, then we and our children and our children's children would be enslaved to Pharaoh in Egypt.

BEE BA DO DUM DUM, BUM BADUM BUM BUH, BAH DUH, BAH DAH DUM DUM, DUM DEDUM DUM DUM DUM DUM. BADA DO DUM DEDUM.

The Seinfeld Words

There are a bunch of words *Seinfeld* invented that have filtered into the modern lexicon. Some more famous ones include: Yada Yada[C65] (when you skip over part of a story); anti-dentite[C66] (when someone is biased against dentists); re-gifter[C67] (someone who

THE (UNOFFICIAL) SEINFELD HAGGADAH

The matzot should stay untucked for the duration of maggid. Some matzot untucked and some tucked is acceptable as well, but it's easier if they are all untucked.

עֲבָדִים הָיִינוּ

עֲבָדִים הָיִינוּ לְפַרְעֹה בְּמִצְרָיִם, וַיּוֹצִיאֵנוּ ה' אֱלֹהֵינוּ מִשָּׁם בְּיָד חֲזָקָה וּבִזְרֹעַ נְטוּיָה. וְאִלּוּ לֹא הוֹצִיא הַקָּדוֹשׁ בָּרוּךְ הוּא אֶת אֲבוֹתֵינוּ מִמִּצְרַיִם, הֲרֵי אָנוּ וּבָנֵינוּ וּבְנֵי בָנֵינוּ מְשֻׁעְבָּדִים הָיִינוּ לְפַרְעֹה בְּמִצְרָיִם.

בִּי בָה דוּ דוּם דוּם, בּוּם בְּדוּם בּוּם בֹּן, בָּה דוּ, בָּה דָה דוּם דוּם, דוּם דוּדוּם דוּם דוּם דוּם דוּם דוּם. בָּדָה דוּ דוּם דְדוּם.

gifts gifts that have already been received); close talker[C68] (a person who talks too close to other people); Shiksapeal[C69] (the particular appeal of a non-Jewish woman to a Jewish man); and the "master of my domain" (see: "The Contest[C70]"). While these words are largely understood within the context of a conversation, they are inextricably linked to *Seinfeld*.

In his groundbreaking academic work "Inconsistencies in the Torah," Rabbi Dr. Joshua Berman argues that the Biblical wording used to describe the Exodus is unique to ancient Egypt. For example: in Avadim Hayinu, the phrase "with a strong hand and an outstretched arm" is unique to Egyptian manuscripts. The term is not found in any other ancient Near Eastern writings. Similarly, the Song of the Sea, referenced later in Maggid, reflects an extraordinary similarity to the Kadesh Poem of Ramses, a famous Egyptian poem cataloging Ramses' victory in Kadesh, during the Biblical time period. The Tabernacle, which the Jews will build soon after they leave Egypt, closely resembles Ramses' battle compound as seen in bas reliefs. While these similarities between the words the Torah uses and their Egyptian counterparts do not prove that the Exodus story took place, it does seem to indicate the Godly Author of the Biblical story was present at the time. Just like we would assume someone who used *Seinfeld* words watches *Seinfeld* or was at least present for its existence, Berman assumes the same with the Exodus, making us more confident when we say "We were slaves to Pharaoh in Egypt…"

And even if we were all sages, all discerning, all elders, all knowledgeable about the Torah, it would be our duty to tell the story of the exodus from Egypt. And anyone who adds, and doesn't Yada Yada[19], and spends extra time in telling the story of the exodus from Egypt, behold they are praiseworthy.

═ BEE BA DO DUM DUM, BUM BADUM BUM BUH, BAH DUH, BAH DAH DUM DUM, DUM DEDUM DUM DUM DUM DUM. BADA DO DUM DEDUM. ═

The Neverending Talking

Right when we begin to talk about the Exodus, the Haggadah tells us that each and every one of us must talk about the Exodus story. Irregardless of our personal backgrounds, it is each person who attends the Seder's responsibility to verbalize the story out loud and as much as possible. Rav Yosef Dov Soleveitchik (in Redemption, Prayer, Talmud Torah) notes the following:

"The slave is deprived of meaningfulness of speech. He lives in silence - if such a meaningless existence is called life. He has no message to deliver. In contrast with the slave, a free man bears a message, has a good deal to tell, and is eager to convey his life story to anyone who cares to listen."

Our ability to speak freely and meaningfully about the Exodus demonstrates our freedom. If the ability to speak one's mind is a symbol of freedom, no one is more free than Kramer. Multiple times throughout the show, Kramer speaks his mind in a completely inappropriate fashion. In "The Phone Message[C71]," he brings up Jerry and his girlfriend's recent argument about the cotton Dockers commercial (she likes it, he can't understand how anyone could), which ends up leading to their breakup. In "The Apartment[C72]," Kramer suggests Jerry should lend Elaine $5000 to get an apartment in the building, when lending large sums of money to friends is awkward, and Jerry would prefer her not to live in the same building. In "The Nose Job[C73]," Kramer suggests to George's girlfriend that she would look much prettier if she got a nose job. Kramer speaks his mind so freely that in "The Kiss Hello[C74]," Elaine introduces him to her friend Wendy in the hopes that Kramer will tell her to change

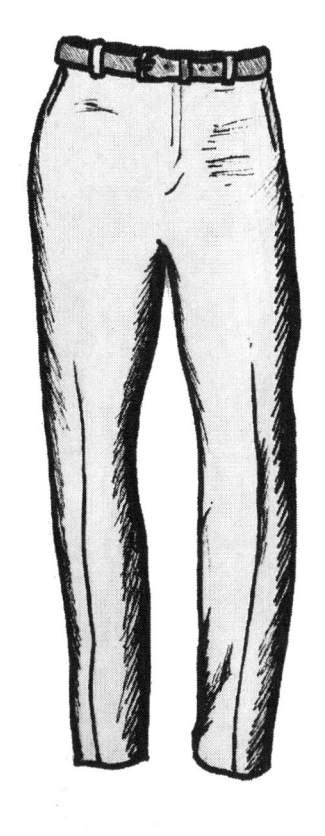

וַאֲפִילוּ כֻּלָּנוּ חֲכָמִים כֻּלָּנוּ נְבוֹנִים כֻּלָּנוּ זְקֵנִים כֻּלָּנוּ יוֹדְעִים אֶת הַתּוֹרָה, מִצְוָה עָלֵינוּ לְסַפֵּר בִּיצִיאַת מִצְרָיִם. וְכָל הַמַּרְבֶּה לְסַפֵּר בִּיצִיאַת מִצְרָיִם הֲרֵי זֶה מְשֻׁבָּח.

בי בה דו דום דום, בום בדום בום בו, בה דו, בה דה דום דום, דום דדום דום דה דום דום. בדה דו דום דדום.

her hairdo, which she thinks is old fashioned. (Of course, Kramer happens to love her hair and tells Wendy to keep it.)

There are also some downsides to Kramer's complete candidness. In "The Cartoon[C75]," Kramer gets into trouble when she accidentally offends Sally Weaver, a new standup comic. Jerry told Kramer that he doesn't like her act and she should quit show business. Clearly, Jerry's opinion was not meant for her ears, but Kramer tells her anyways. Kramer realizes his inability to be quiet, so he tries to stop talking, but his silence ends up hurting him also. Eventually, Kramer lands in more trouble with Sally when he can not keep being silent and blurts out a host of critiques. While Kramer realizes that while speaking his mind can sometimes cause problems, being silent is like being a slave. While we surely should surely be more courteous at the Seder than Kramer usually is, the idiosyncratic lead also demonstrates the freedom that accompanies speaking one's mind.

THE HAGGADAH ABOUT NOTHING

STORY OF THE FIVE TALKERS

It happened once on Passover that Rabbi Eliezer (the close talker[20]), Rabbi Yehoshua (the lip reader[21]), Rabbi Elazar ben Azariah (the high talker[22]), Rabbi Akiva (the long talker[23]) and Rabbi Tarfon (the low talker[24]) were reclining in Bnei Brak and were telling the story of the exodus from Egypt that whole night (at least they didn't have an AIDS walk in the morning[25]), until their students came and said to them, "The time of reciting the morning Shema has arrived."

═ BEE BA DO DUM DUM, BUM BADUM BUM BUH, BAH DUH, BAH DAH DUM DUM, DUM DEDUM DUM DUM DUM DUM. BADA DO DUM DEDUM. ═

The Optimism of George

George is an extraordinarily pessimistic person. He does not have a high opinion of himself, and it shows. In "The Finale[C76]," when the private jet to Paris the four main characters are on has turbulence and they think it might all be over George says: "Just when I was doing great... I told you God wouldn't let me be successful." In "The Millenium[C77]," when George is trying but failing to get fired from his job at the Yankees, he says, "All right. I guess I just have to pick myself up, dust myself off, and throw myself right back down again!" In "The Lip Reader[C78]," when George's girlfriend tries to break up with him kindly, he responds, "You're giving me the 'It's not you, it's me' routine? I invented 'It's not you, it's me.' Nobody tells me it's them, not me. If it's anybody, it's me." In "The Old Man[C79]," George thinks the best thing he does is quitting: "Yeah, I'm a great quitter. It's one of the few things I do well. I come from a long line of quitters. My father was a quitter, my grandfather was a quitter... I was raised to give up." In "The Masseuse[C80]," he falls in love with a woman who hates him: "This woman hates me so much, I'm starting to like her."

Rabbi Kenneth Brander, President and Rosh Yeshiva of Ohr Torah Stone, notes that Rabbi Akiva, the Talmudic sage, is the king of optimism, ergo the opposite of George. In this group of five Rabbis,

THE (UNOFFICIAL) SEINFELD HAGGADAH

מעשה שהיה בבני ברק

מַעֲשֶׂה בְּרַבִּי אֱלִיעֶזֶר וְרַבִּי יְהוֹשֻׁעַ וְרַבִּי אֶלְעָזָר בֶּן־עֲזַרְיָה וְרַבִּי עֲקִיבָא וְרַבִּי טַרְפוֹן שֶׁהָיוּ מְסֻבִּין בִּבְנֵי בְרַק וְהָיוּ מְסַפְּרִים בִּיצִיאַת מִצְרַיִם כָּל אוֹתוֹ הַלַּיְלָה, עַד שֶׁבָּאוּ תַלְמִידֵיהֶם וְאָמְרוּ לָהֶם, "רַבּוֹתֵינוּ הִגִּיעַ זְמַן קְרִיאַת שְׁמַע שֶׁל שַׁחֲרִית."

בִּי בַּה דוּ דוּם דוּם, בּוּם בַדוּם בּוּם בּוּ, בַּה דוּ, בַּה דַה דוּם דוּם, דוּם דַדוּם דוּם דוּם דוּם דוּם. בַדַה דוּ דוּם דדוּם.

Rabbi Akia has argued with all of them where he is optimistic and they are pessimistic. With the three Rabbis other than Rabbi Tarfon, while on a stroll near the ruins of the Temple, they see a fox roaming. The other Rabbis are distraught, but Rabbi Akiva laughs. Rabbi Akiva is optimistic that since these negative prophecies about the Temple destruction happened, surely the positive ones of the Temple being rebuilt will happen too (end of Tractate Makkot).

Rabbi Akiva argues with Rabbi Tarfon about the text of the blessing over the fourth cup of wine at the end of the Seder. Rabbi Tarfon's formulation focuses only on the past, while Rabbi Akiva's formulation adds parts about Temple being rebuilt and the future time when God will save us. (We use Rabbi Akiva's formulation in the Haggadah.) This Seder of the five Rabbis, happens in Bnei Brak, Rabbi Akiva's hometown because the conversation is Rabbi Akiva's. It is about his optimism and telling us that we too should be optimistic that our future redemption will come. This is why they talk about the Exodus until morning time, when they are told it is time to say the morning Shema. They discuss the Exodus through the entire long difficult and murky night and exile, and are still doing so until the morning when there is light and a new freedom. It is the optimism of Rabbi Akiva that leads us through the dark night to the break of dawn. The Haggadah has us acknowledge that we should be

THE HAGGADAH ABOUT NOTHING

Rabbi Elazar ben Azariah said, "Behold I am like a man of seventy years, but still in perfect health, he works out, he's vibrant[26], and I have not merited to understand why the exodus from Egypt should be said at night until Ben Zoma explained it, as it is stated (Deuteronomy 16:3), 'In order that you remember the day of your going out from the land of Egypt all the days of your life;' 'the days of your life' indicates that the remembrance be invoked during the days, 'all the days of your life' indicates that the remembrance be invoked also during the nights." Those all are the everyday Exodus balloons[27]. But the Sages say, "'the days of your life' indicates that the remembrance be invoked in this world, 'all the days of your life' indicates that the remembrance be invoked also in the days of the Messiah."

THE FOUR SONS

Blessed be the Place (to be[28]),
Blessed be He;
Blessed be the One
who Gave the Torah
to His people Israel, Blessed be He.

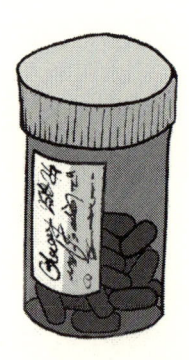

══ BEE BA DO DUM DUM, BUM BADUM BUM BUH, BAH DUH, BAH DAH DUM DUM, DUM DEDUM DUM DUM DUM DUM. BADA DO DUM DEDUM. ══

optimistic about the future and no matter how bleak the world looks, we will be saved in the future. George has the opposite approach, now matter how good the world is, he assumes it will become worse. The Exodus story shows us that God does not have George's approach with us and we should also not embrace that approach with Him.

46 — MAGGID

אָמַר רַבִּי אֶלְעָזָר בֶּן־עֲזַרְיָה
"הֲרֵי אֲנִי כְּבֶן שִׁבְעִים שָׁנָה
וְלֹא זָכִיתִי שֶׁתֵּאָמֵר
יְצִיאַת מִצְרַיִם בַּלֵּילוֹת
עַד שֶׁדְּרָשָׁהּ בֶּן זוֹמָא,
שֶׁנֶּאֱמַר (דברים טז, ג): 'לְמַעַן תִּזְכֹּר
אֶת יוֹם צֵאתְךָ מֵאֶרֶץ מִצְרַיִם
כֹּל יְמֵי חַיֶּיךָ.'
'יְמֵי חַיֶּיךָ' הַיָּמִים.
'כֹּל יְמֵי חַיֶּיךָ' הַלֵּילוֹת.
וַחֲכָמִים אוֹמְרִים:
"יְמֵי חַיֶּיךָ' הָעוֹלָם הַזֶּה.
'כֹּל יְמֵי חַיֶּיךָ' לְהָבִיא לִימוֹת הַמָּשִׁיחַ."

כנגד ארבעה בנים

בָּרוּךְ הַמָּקוֹם, בָּרוּךְ הוּא,
בָּרוּךְ שֶׁנָּתַן תּוֹרָה
לְעַמּוֹ יִשְׂרָאֵל, בָּרוּךְ הוּא.

בי בה דו דום, בום בדום בום בו, בה דו, בה דה דום דום, דום דדום דום דום דום. בדה דו דום דדום.

The Makom of Pharmacists

Jerry doesn't understand Pharmacists' status in society. In "The Nose Job[C81]," he muses:

Can you give me an explanation as to why the pharmacist has to be two-and-a-half feet up above everybody else? ...Oh no, he's gotta be two-and-a-half feet up. "Look out, everybody, I'm working with pills. Spread out, give me some room." The only hard part of his whole job that I could see is typing everything onto that little tiny label. He has to try and get all the words on there, keep the paper in the– it's a little piece of paper, in the roller of the typewriter. Oh no, he's gotta be two-and-a-half feet up. "Yeah, I'd like to get this prescription filled." "Alright, and you wait down there, only I'm allowed up here."

And Jerry is right, no? And while pharmacists are high up to prevent theft, having them on a higher physical plane does make us feel a sense of higher status. Regardless of the reason we place the

== BEE BA DO DUM DUM, BUM BADUM BUM BUH, BAH DUH, BAH DAH DUM DUM, DUM DEDUM DUM DUM DUM DUM. BADA DO DUM DEDUM. ==

Corresponding to four children did the Torah speak; one who is wise, one who is impulsive, one who is simple and one who doesn't know to ask.

What does the wise child say? "You know people think I'm wise, but I'm not really wise[29]" and "'What are these testimonies, statutes (or statues[30]) and judgments that the Lord, our God, commanded you?' (Deuteronomy 6:20)" And you will say to him, as per the laws of the Passover sacrifice, "We may not eat an afikoman, a dessert or other foods eaten after the meal (especially if they are in a trash can, even if they are on top[31]), after we are finished eating the Passover sacrifice. (Mishnah Pesachim 10:8)"

What does the impulsive child say? "'What is this worship to you?' (Exodus 12:26)" meaning for you and not for him. And since he excluded himself from the community, he shows he denies a main principle of the Jewish faith. And accordingly, you will blunt his teeth with a schtickle of fluoride[32] and say to him, "'For the sake of this, did the Lord do this for me in

48 — MAGGID

THE (UNOFFICIAL) SEINFELD HAGGADAH

pharmacists high up, the effect of placing them higher up is the same.

Rambam, also known as Maimonides, in his Guide to the Perplexed (1:8), explains that we call God "Hamakom," the place, referring to the exalted special place that God inhabits. Rambam writes that Blessed is the Place (hamakom) means: "Blessed be the Lord according to the exalted nature of His existence," and wherever makom is applied to God, it expresses the same idea, namely, the distinguished position of His existence, to which nothing is equal or comparable. Even on a night when we see ourselves as royalty, God is still considered to be exalted above, and worthy of our praise. In the Haggadah, we reserve the status that Jerry assumes secular society sometimes gives to pharmacists, to God alone.

בי בה דו דום דום, בום בדום בום בן, בה דו, בה דה דום דום, דום דדום דום דום דום דום. בדה דו דום דדום.

כְּנֶגֶד אַרְבָּעָה בָנִים דִּבְּרָה תוֹרָה:
אֶחָד חָכָם, וְאֶחָד רָשָׁע,
וְאֶחָד תָּם, וְאֶחָד שֶׁאֵינוֹ יוֹדֵעַ לִשְׁאוֹל.

חָכָם מָה הוּא אוֹמֵר?
"מָה הָעֵדוֹת וְהַחֻקִּים
וְהַמִּשְׁפָּטִים אֲשֶׁר צִוָּה
ה' אֱלֹהֵינוּ אֶתְכֶם?' (דברים ו, כ)"
וְאַף אַתָּה אֱמוֹר לוֹ כְּהִלְכוֹת הַפֶּסַח:
"אֵין מַפְטִירִין אַחַר הַפֶּסַח אֲפִיקוֹמָן. (משנה פסחים י, ח)"

רָשָׁע מָה הוּא אוֹמֵר?
"'מָה הָעֲבוֹדָה הַזֹּאת לָכֶם.' (שמות יב, כו)"

מגיד — 49

my going out of Egypt' (Exodus 13:8)." 'For me' and not 'for him!' If he had been there, he would not have been saved.

What does the simple child say? "'What is this?' (Exodus 13:14)" And you will say to him, "'With the strength of His hand did the Lord take us out from Egypt, from the house of slaves' (Exodus 13:14)."

And regarding the one who doesn't know to ask, you will open the conversation for him. As it is stated, "And you will speak to your son on that day saying, for the sake of this, did the Lord do this for me in my going out of Egypt. (Exodus 13:8)"

═ BEE BA DO DUM DUM, BUM BADUM BUM BUH, BAH DUH, BAH DAH DUM DUM, DUM DEDUM DUM DUM DUM DUM. BADA DO DUM DEDUM. ═

The Four Humorous Ones

Yes, you probably knew this was coming, the four main characters of *Seinfeld* can be characterized as the four sons in the Haggadah. Before we compare them to the characters at hand, we first need to offer a general explanation of the sons. The four sons are clearly meant as allegory, fictional paradigms of personality traits that are present at the Seder. Looking back into history, the idea of four personality types was far reaching. Around the time the Haggadah was written, these four prototypes were most famously found in the four humors Greek thought.

In Greek philosophy, there are four secretions in the body: black bile, blood, phlegm, yellow bile. These secretions were said to control one's personality. The more a person had of any one secretion the more they had the corresponding personality traits. While there are many explanations of the four humors, there are certain thematic threads that follow through. Black Bile is honor bound and loyal, perfectionist to a fault. Yellow bile is all over the place, unfocused. Phlegm is shy, pragmatic, and anxious. They are lazy and can fall into

THE (UNOFFICIAL) SEINFELD HAGGADAH

לָכֶם – וְלֹא לוֹ.
וּלְפִי שֶׁהוֹצִיא אֶת עַצְמוֹ מִן הַכְּלָל כָּפַר בְּעִקָּר.
וְאַף אַתָּה הַקְהֵה אֶת שִׁנָּיו וֶאֱמוֹר לוֹ:
"'בַּעֲבוּר זֶה עָשָׂה ה' לִי בְּצֵאתִי מִמִּצְרָיִם.' (שמות יג, ח)
'לִי' וְלֹא 'לוֹ.' אִלּוּ הָיָה שָׁם, לֹא הָיָה נִגְאָל.

תָּם מָה הוּא אוֹמֵר?
"'מַה זֹּאת?' (שמות יג, יד)
וְאָמַרְתָּ אֵלָיו, "בְּחֹזֶק יָד
הוֹצִיאָנוּ ה' מִמִּצְרַיִם מִבֵּית עֲבָדִים.' (שמות יג, יד)"

וְשֶׁאֵינוֹ יוֹדֵעַ לִשְׁאוֹל,
אַתְּ פְּתַח לוֹ, שֶׁנֶּאֱמַר,
"וְהִגַּדְתָּ לְבִנְךָ בַּיּוֹם הַהוּא לֵאמֹר,
בַּעֲבוּר זֶה עָשָׂה ה' לִי בְּצֵאתִי מִמִּצְרָיִם. (שמות יג, ח)"

בִּי בָּה דוּ דוּם דוּם, בּוּם בָּדוּם בּוּם בּוֹ, בָּה דוּ, בָּה דָּה דוּם דוּם, דוּם דָּדוּם דוּם דוּם דוּם דוּם. בָּדָה דוּ דוּם דָּדוּם.

the background. Blood is sensitive and passionate. They act on whims in an impulsive fashion. During the Greek empire, ancient doctors would try to help a person by taking out some of one fluid to realign the body. If they were too passionate, the doctor would bloodlet. If they were too unfocused, the doctor would take out yellow bile, and so on. While modern medicine has rejected the idea of these four fluids controlling our personality, the concept of the four personality types can help us understand the four sons of the Haggadah.

מגיד

The chacham (wise son) is black bile. The chacham asks about the rules of Pesach night. They want to follow the rules perfectly and please their father. The answer given to the chacham is therefore appropriate. We tell them about the minor law that you can only eat the afikoman (the matzah "dessert") until Halakhic midnight. The tam, simple son, is the phlegm. They ask a fairly shy and pragmatic question: "What's this?" The tam similarly gets a pragmatic answer that we do the Seder because God took us out of Egypt. The sheeino yodeah lishol (son who doesn't know how to ask) is the yellow bile. They are not focused, you need to open up the conversation for them. Lastly, the rasha (usually translated as wicked son) is the blood.

In this paradigm, the rasha is not wicked, but passionate and acts on whims be they positive or negative. They get upset in the moment because of how much work Pesach is ("What is this 'work' to you?"), and ask an inappropriately phrased question. The answer of blunting his teeth is taking away his fangs, taking away the passionate intensity, taking away his "hand" as George would say. In Jewish sources, the term "rasha" does not always mean someone who was wicked, but someone who lets their passion sway them. In the beginning of the Exodus story, Moses meets two jews fighting (Exodus 2:13). The Midrash (in Shemot Rabbah) understands this to mean that one was about to hit the other, and therefore the Torah calls him Rasha (wicked). Therefore, only the Jews who were willing to leave and were faithful were taken out of Egypt. It is those that were able to be persistent and not lose hope when things got difficult that were worthy of redemption. The Rasha would not have been redeemed.

These same four types of people are our four characters in *Seinfeld*. Jerry is clearly the chacham who cares deeply about the rules. He is always investigating them trying to understand what the rules, written and unwritten are. He is constantly discussing the minutiae of how people should and shouldn't act in polite society. He is a neat freak who searches for perfection in his house and his jokes. He is loyal to his parents; his first thought after making some big money is buying his father a Cadillac[C82]. Kramer is very clearly the sheeino yodea lishol. He is not focused and moves from preoccupation to preoccupation. George, is the Tam. George is pragmatic and lazy. Most notably, Jerry describes how hard George works to stay on unemployment. His "summer of George" is completely wasted on the couch in front of a TV. Kramer understands George's simple nature the most. In "The Secret Code[C83]," Kramer gets very close to guessing his ATM code, "Bosco," because he understands George is a simple guy that cares about his simple temptations, like sweets. In "The Cafe[C84]," when Elaine wants to know why Geroge is wearing cologne he says: "why must I always be the focal point of attention? Let me just be, let me just live." George wishes to live simply and be left alone. Elaine is therefore the Rasha. She is by no means wicked, at least no more wicked than the other characters, but she is particularly impulsive. Her patented "Get Out" shove is indicative of her impulsiveness. Her entire relationship with Puddy, her on and off again boyfriend, is as well. She breaks up and gets back together with him on a whim and is clearly very aggressive towards him. When she and Puddy go to Europe for a trip, Kramer's reaction is "Boy, a month in Europe with Elaine. That guy's coming home in a body bag[C85]." While Elaine is not any more wicked than the other main characters persay, she certainly is the scariest one, the one you most fear might raise their hand against another, even if she wouldn't hit.

This foursome is not unique to *Seinfeld*. The same four paradigms can be found in *Sex and the City, The Wizard of Oz, Teenage Mutant Ninja Turtles, Ghostbusters*, and many more. These shows work so well because every person can relate to one of the characters because they are the building blocks of personality. Every person is really all of the sons at the Seder, but each person likely resonates with one in particular. This set of characters makes *Seinfeld* work so well. It also makes everyone try and feel welcome at the Seder. The Seder is for the entire Jewish nation, and everyone is invited no matter if you relate to Jerry, Kramer, George, or Elaine.

*Note: initial thought of humors connection to TV from the youtube channel Cracked: After Hours.

YECHOL ME'ROSH CHODESH

It could be that one would have to discuss the Exodus from Rosh Chodesh Nissan. However, we learn otherwise, since it is stated, "on that day." If it is written with an astronaut pen[33] "on that day," it could be from while it is still day before the night of the fifteenth of Nissan. However, since it is stated, "for the sake of this." I didn't say "for the sake of this" except that it be observed when this matzah and maror are resting in front of you, meaning on the night of the fifteenth only.

IN THE BEGINNING
OUR FATHERS WERE IDOL WORSHIPERS

From the beginning, our ancestors were idol worshipers. And now, the exalted One has brought us close to His worship, as it is stated (Joshua 24:2-4), "Yehoshua said to the whole people, so said the Lord, God of Israel, 'Over the river did your ancestors dwell from always, Terach the father

═ BEE BA DO DUM DUM, BUM BADUM BUM BUH, BAH DUH, BAH DAH DUM DUM, DUM DEDUM DUM DUM DUM DUM. BADA DO DUM DEDUM. ═

The Not Tuesday

Newman would likely agree that Pesach is not supposed to be like a Tuesday, it's supposed to have a feel. In "The Sniffing Accountant[C86]," while on a stakeout with Jerry, Kramer and Newman have a conversation about how days "feel":

KRAMER: What's today?
NEWMAN: It's Thursday.
KRAMER: Really? Feels like Tuesday.
NEWMAN: Tuesday has no feel. Monday has a feel, Friday has a feel, Sunday has a feel....
KRAMER: I feel Tuesday and Wednesday...

54 — MAGGID

יכול מראש חדש

יָכוֹל מֵרֹאשׁ חֹדֶשׁ?
תַּלְמוּד לוֹמַר "בַּיּוֹם הַהוּא."
אִי "בַּיּוֹם הַהוּא" יָכוֹל מִבְּעוֹד יוֹם?
תַּלְמוּד לוֹמַר "בַּעֲבוּר זֶה"
"בַּעֲבוּר זֶה" לֹא אָמַרְתִּי,
אֶלָּא בְּשָׁעָה שֶׁיֵּשׁ מַצָּה וּמָרוֹר מֻנָּחִים לְפָנֶיךָ.

מתחילה עובדי עבודה זרה היו אבותינו

מִתְּחִלָּה עוֹבְדֵי עֲבוֹדָה זָרָה הָיוּ אֲבוֹתֵינוּ, וְעַכְשָׁיו קֵרְבָנוּ הַמָּקוֹם לַעֲבֹדָתוֹ, שֶׁנֶּאֱמַר (יהושע כד, ב-ד): "וַיֹּאמֶר יְהוֹשֻׁעַ אֶל־כָּל־הָעָם, כֹּה אָמַר ה' אֱלֹהֵי יִשְׂרָאֵל: 'בְּעֵבֶר הַנָּהָר יָשְׁבוּ אֲבוֹתֵיכֶם מֵעוֹלָם, תֶּרַח אֲבִי אַבְרָהָם וַאֲבִי נָחוֹר, וַיַּעַבְדוּ אֱלֹהִים אֲחֵרִים.

―― בי בה דו דום דום, בום בדום בום בו, בה דו, בה דה דום דום, דום דדום דום דום דום. בדה דו דום דדום. ――

Pesach is supposed to have a direct feel. This is why the Seder must happen on the night of Pesach. While we do remember the Exodus on other days, we have to do it when the foods (matza, maror etc.) are in front of us on Seder night. The Seder is more than an intellectual exercise, not just something to talk about, but a feeling that is being conveyed. The Exodus story is our story, one we feel is happening to us on Seder night. We will later read in the Haggadah that "In every generation, a person must view themselves as if they had gone out of Egypt." All the aspects of the Seder are supposed to give over a feeling of personal connection to the story that is happening right now.

of Avraham and the father of Nachor, and they worshiped other gods. And I took your father, Avraham, from over the river and I made him walk in all the land of Canaan and I increased his seed (the Abraham name lives on![34]) and I gave him Yitzchak. And I gave to Yitzchak, Yaakov and Esav; and I gave to Esav, Mount Seir to inherit it; and Yaakov and his sons went down to Egypt.'"

═══ BEE BA DO DUM DUM, BUM BADUM BUM BUH, BAH DUH, BAH DAH DUM DUM, DUM DEDUM DUM DUM DUM DUM. BADA DO DUM DEDUM. ═══

The Covenant

It is at this point of the Haggadah where we really learn "what's the deal" on Pesach. Rabbi Shlomo Riskin, an Orthodox Rabbi who founded Lincoln Square Synagogue on the Upper West Side (near Jerry's apartment), notes that the Brit Ben Habetarim (the Covenant between the Parts) was a turning point in Avraham's relationship with God. Until then, Avraham understood the relationship to be a contingent deal. If he kept his side of the deal, then God would be good to him. Avraham, in Genesis 15:7, asks "How will I know that I will inherit the land?" God responds with a covenant. The answer to Avraham's question is not that the land is part of a deal, but that the relationship is covenantal and not contingent on Avraham's offspring's righteousness. The relationship is irrevocable, and never changing.

In "The Engagement[C87]," George and Jerry enter a pact. While it functions much more like a covenant than a deal, they are never explicit about the pact's nature. In this pact, both of them decide to "get their lives together." Jerry is going to call back Melanie, who he broke up with for shushing him, and George is going to call back his long time girlfriend, Susan. Beyond their relationships, they both decide to make big changes to their lives. As Jerry notes about them shooting the breeze in the coffee shop: "What is this? What are we doing? What in God's name are we doing?" That day, George takes strong action and gets engaged to Susan, but Jerry does not. He breaks up with Melanie because she eats her peas one at a time. George feels like Jerry didn't live up to the pact, and is disappointed, but doesn't give up on Jerry. For George, the pact isn't over because

וָאֶקַּח אֶת־אֲבִיכֶם
אֶת־אַבְרָהָם מֵעֵבֶר
הַנָּהָר וָאוֹלֵךְ אוֹתוֹ
בְּכָל־אֶרֶץ כְּנָעַן,
וָאַרְבֶּה אֶת־זַרְעוֹ
וָאֶתֵּן לוֹ אֶת־יִצְחָק,
וָאֶתֵּן לְיִצְחָק
אֶת־יַעֲקֹב
וְאֶת־עֵשָׂו.
וָאֶתֵּן לְעֵשָׂו אֶת־הַר
שֵׂעִיר לָרֶשֶׁת אֹתוֹ,
וְיַעֲקֹב וּבָנָיו
יָרְדוּ מִצְרָיִם."

בי בה דו דום דום, בום בדום בום בו, בה דו, בה דה דום דום, דום דדום דום דום דום. בדה דו דום דדום.

one party didn't follow the rules, the covenant is irrevocable. Their bond endures. George brings it up again when Jerry ends his relationship with "Shmoopy" because the pact is much more than a deal. It can't be reneged from, even if Jerry is trying to. For Jerry, it isn't a covenant, "we just shook hands," he says. Because Jerry always saw it as merely a handshake deal (like the one he makes with Elaine in "The Deal[C88]"), the pact is never really effective to begin with.

    The Brit Ben Habetarim functions as the clarification that George and Jerry never have. Avraham now truly understands that this relationship is much more than a deal between himself and God. God will always be his descendant's guarantor and we will always be his people of the covenant. As Rabbi Riskin ends his sermon: "The Jewish people is the am Ha-brit, the people of the covenant, and all of Jewish History is the practical expression of the Divine-Human encounter." That encounter is more than a deal." It is a pact where both we and God can have "this, that, and the other[C89]."

THE HAGGADAH ABOUT NOTHING

Blessed be the One who keeps His promise to (Bobby, like Paul O'Neill did[35], and to) Israel, blessed be He; since the Holy One, blessed be He, calculated the end of the exile, to do as He said to Avraham, our father, in the Pact[36] between the Pieces, as it is stated (Genesis 15:13-14), "And He said to Avram, 'you should surely know that your seed will be a stranger in a land that is not theirs, and they will enslave them and afflict them four hundred years. And also that nation for which they shall toil will I judge, and afterwards they will go out with much property.'" Saying that He would both take the reservation and hold the reservation[37].

Cover the matzah, lift up the cup, and say:

And it is this that has stood for our ancestors and for us; since it is not only one Newman[38] that has stood against us to destroy us, but rather in each generation, Newmans stand against us to destroy us, but the Holy One, blessed be He, rescues us from their hands.

═ BEE BA DO DUM DUM, BUM BADUM BUM BUH, BAH DUH, BAH DAH DUM DUM, DUM DEDUM DUM DUM DUM DUM. BADA DO DUM DEDUM. ═

The Jujyfruits Gadol

During the Exodus, the Jewish people are leaving a slavery that was intense and lasted 210 years. They leave with miracles upon miracles... and lots of wealth? One would think they would be focused so entirely on leaving, they would forgo anything extra, even if owed. In "The Opposite[C90]," a similar question is asked to Elaine by her boyfriend, Jake Jarmel. When entering the movie theatre to meet Jake, Elaine finds out that Jake was in a car accident and was brought to the hospital. She was a couple steps from the counter so she quickly picks up some Jujyfruit candy for her way. When she gets to the hospital, Jake is not happy when he realizes, and says: "I would think, under the circumstances, it would have sent you running out the building. Apparently, it didn't have any effect on you."

While the two scenarios seem a little similar, the impetus for

THE (UNOFFICIAL) SEINFELD HAGGADAH

בָּרוּךְ שׁוֹמֵר הַבְטָחָתוֹ לְיִשְׂרָאֵל, בָּרוּךְ הוּא. שֶׁהַקָּדוֹשׁ בָּרוּךְ הוּא חִשַּׁב אֶת־הַקֵּץ, לַעֲשׂוֹת כְּמוֹ שֶׁאָמַר לְאַבְרָהָם אָבִינוּ בִּבְרִית בֵּין הַבְּתָרִים, שֶׁנֶּאֱמַר (בראשית טו, יג-יד): "וַיֹּאמֶר לְאַבְרָם, 'יָדֹעַ תֵּדַע כִּי־גֵר יִהְיֶה זַרְעֲךָ בְּאֶרֶץ לֹא לָהֶם, וַעֲבָדוּם וְעִנּוּ אֹתָם אַרְבַּע מֵאוֹת שָׁנָה. וְגַם אֶת־הַגּוֹי אֲשֶׁר יַעֲבֹדוּ דָּן אָנֹכִי וְאַחֲרֵי־כֵן יֵצְאוּ בִּרְכֻשׁ גָּדוֹל.'"

Cover the matzah, lift up the cup, and say:

וְהִיא שֶׁעָמְדָה לַאֲבוֹתֵינוּ וְלָנוּ. שֶׁלֹּא אֶחָד בִּלְבַד עָמַד עָלֵינוּ לְכַלּוֹתֵנוּ, אֶלָּא שֶׁבְּכָל דּוֹר וָדוֹר עוֹמְדִים עָלֵינוּ לְכַלּוֹתֵנוּ, וְהַקָּדוֹשׁ בָּרוּךְ הוּא מַצִּילֵנוּ מִיָּדָם.

בִּי בַּה דוּ דוּם דוּם, בּוּם בְּדוּם בּוּם בְּן, בַּה דוּ, בַּה דַה דוּם דוּם, דוּם דְּדוּם דוּם דוּם דוּם דוּם. בַּדַה דוּ דוּם דְּדוּם.

the two takings could not be different. Elaine really does stop to get Jujyfruit, and we even find out later she stopped for popcorn too. Elaine's motivation was her hunger. She does somewhat rush out, but still decides herself to stop for a snack. The impetus for the "rechush gadol" (great wealth) couldn't be more different. The people were ready to "run out of the building," but God had more ideas in mind. God promised Avraham they would leave with great wealth, partly because the wealth itself is a way for them to feel like free people, but also as a show of God's strength over Egypt. God sees that the Jewish people are not going to stop for "Jujyfruits," but they have to show God's true redemption.

The Vehi Sheamda Tone

How things are said can strongly change their meaning. In "The Alternate Side[C91]," Kramer gets a line in a Wooden Allen movie: "These pretzels are making me thirsty." The group doesn't like how Kramer is saying it, so they all take a shot at the line. How they each say it is dramatically different. Jerry says it in a jovial way that is so central to his character because he "can't not be funny[C92]." George recites the line in an exasperated way because he is frustrated trying to move a lot of cars for alternate side parking for a living. Elaine delivers it matter of factly, as she is staying even keel about to break up with her boyfriend who is much older than her. Similarly, in "The Seinfeld Chronicles[C93]," Jerry is unsure of what his relationship is with Laura who is visiting NYC for a couple days. Jerry and George decide that they can determine her intentions from her greeting to Jerry. The plan falls apart when she does the "surprise-blindfold-greeting," leaving them confused. In "The Fix Up[C94]," Jerry and Elaine are trying to set up George and Elaine's friend Cynthia, when Elaine says she doesn't want to start setting people up with George, Jerry says: "well why wouldn't you start with George? You think she's too good for George?" Her tone makes Jerry assume she is making a large statement about George, changing the conversation dramatically. In "The Mom and Pop Store[C95]," Jerry isn't sure if he is invited to Tim Whatley's Thanksgiving party. Elaine, who Tim Whately called Jerry to ask for her number and was invited to the party, tries to find out if Jerry is invited by asking Tim "What should Jerry bring?," to which he responds "Why would Jerry bring anything?" To Jerry, this response is completely dependant on how it was said and he and Elaine have the following conversation:

> JERRY: Alright, but let me ask you this question.
> ELAINE: What?
> JERRY: Which word did he emphasize? Did he say, "Why would Jerry bring anything?" or, "Why would Jerry bring anything?" You emphasize "Jerry" or "bring."
> ELAINE: I think he emphasized "would."

In this conversation, as with the pretzels line, the airport pickup, and the fix up, how things are said dramatically changes the meaning. If Whately emphasized "bring" then he expects Jerry to come but doesn't expect a gift, if "Jerry" then Jerry is likely not invited.

Rabbi Josh Botwinick, Rabbi at OU-Mizrachi-JLIC in IDC-Herzliya and also happens to be my brother-in-law, observes that how Vehi Sheamda is sung changes its meaning dramatically. In the old time traditional tune, the high point of the song is "Elah Shebechol Dor Vador Omdim Aleinu Lechaloteinu" that in every generation our enemies stand up to destroy us. This makes sense as the focus throughout Jewish history, where persecution has largely been the theme, even if we are saved. Distinctly, in 2008, Yaakov Shwekey came out with a very different Vehi Sheamda. Its focus is not on our persecution, but on how Hashem saves us constantly. It's high point is "VeHakadosh Baruch Hu Matzileinu Miyadam" that "God saves us from their hands." This upbeat point of view is far more appropriate in the modern age. We live in prosperity in America and throughout the world, and have a Jewish state in the State of Israel. Anti-Semitism still certainly exists, and has grown stronger since then, but it is certainly a time for Jews to be thankful to God for our relative comfort. Even though in both songs the words are the same, the central point of the song changes the meaning, by changing its focus.

Both interpretations of this passage are true in the Haggadah. We are focusing both on how we are in need of being saved like in every generation, no matter how good we have it, but also how God saves us. They are two sides of the same coin. It is for this reason, at our Seders in the Reinstein home we have been singing both tunes.

THE HAGGADAH ABOUT NOTHING
FIRST FRUITS DECLARATION

Come and learn what Lavan the Aramean sought to do to Yaakov, our father. For Pharaoh only decreed the death of the male children but Lavan sought to destroy us all. As it is stated (Deuteronomy 26:5), **"An Aramean was destroying my father and he went down to Egypt, and he resided there with a small number and he became there a nation, great, powerful and numerous."**

BEE BA DO DUM DUM, BUM BADUM BUM BUH, BAH DUH, BAH DAH DUM DUM, DUM DEDUM DUM DUM DUM DUM. BADA DO DUM DEDUM.

The Going Out

The gang really doesn't like to "go out and learn." Throughout the series, they spend the majority of their time in Jerry's apartment or the coffee shop. In "The Big Salad[C96]," Jerry and Elaine complain about going out on dates and have the following discussion:

> JERRY: People on dates shouldn't even be allowed out in public.
> ELAINE: You can say that again.
> JERRY: It's embarrassing for them. It's painful for us to watch. I'm going out with someone later, I'm not even taking her out of the house.
> ELAINE: Good for you.
> JERRY: I don't need a bunch of people staring at us.
> ELAINE: Right on baby.

They both would rather stay in the apartment when dating than go out and see the world. Similarly, in "The Summer of George[C97]," George's idea of really "getting out there" is reading a book "from beginning to end, in that order" and playing Frisbee golf. What does he end up doing? Lying in his apartment biting off a hunk of cheese "like it's an apple." Even Kramer, who is constantly going on antics, has a sedentary philosophy. When Kramer is bored watching TV, Jerry asks him: "Why don't you go out? It's nice out." to which Kramer replies: "Oh.. no. There's nothing out there for me." In fact, the entire series begins with this sedentary idea. In "The Seinfeld Chronicles[C98]," the first episode of the show, Jerry muses in his introductory standup that people love to "go out," but whenever people are out, they just

צֵא וּלְמַד

צֵא וּלְמַד מַה בִּקֵּשׁ לָבָן הָאֲרַמִּי לַעֲשׂוֹת לְיַעֲקֹב אָבִינוּ: שֶׁפַּרְעֹה לֹא גָזַר אֶלָּא עַל הַזְּכָרִים, וְלָבָן בִּקֵּשׁ לַעֲקֹר אֶת־הַכֹּל. שֶׁנֶּאֱמַר (דברים כו, ה): "אֲרַמִּי אֹבֵד אָבִי, וַיֵּרֶד מִצְרַיְמָה וַיָּגָר שָׁם בִּמְתֵי מְעָט, וַיְהִי שָׁם לְגוֹי גָּדוֹל, עָצוּם, וָרָב."

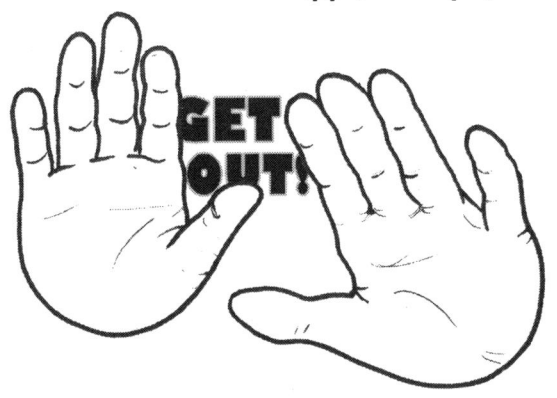

בִּי בָּה דוּ דוּם דוּם, בּוּם בְּדוּם בּוּם בּוּ, בָּה דוּ, בָּה דָּה דוּם דוּם, דוּם דְּדוּם דוּם דוּם דוּם דוּם. בָּדָה דוּ דוּם דְּדוּם.

want to get back.

    Judaism is clearly a religion of tzei ulemad, go out and learn. The part of the Haggadah we are up to is written in a way that is usually reserved for indoors in the Beit Midrash, quoting verses from the text and expounding them. Yet, the Haggadah starts this part of the Haggadah by saying go out and learn and then quoting a first person narrative from Deuteronomy ("An Aramean was destroying my father"). The Haggadah is therefore noting that even when we learn the Exodus from the text, it cannot only be from the text. The Exodus is primarily experiential, it is something you "go out" and do. Rabbi Yosef Adler, Rabbi at Rinat in Teaneck, NJ and my Rebbe in Torah Academy of Bergen County where he serves as Rosh Yeshiva, notes that this is particularly true in hard times. After the flood in Genesis, Noah needs to be told to "leave" the ark. After the destruction, there is an instinct to stay inside, to burrow, but it is precisely then when it is most important to go out, to assert yourself.

    In his famous essay "Rupture and Reconstruction," Rabbi Haym

"And he went down to Egypt" — this means compelled by the Divine decree.

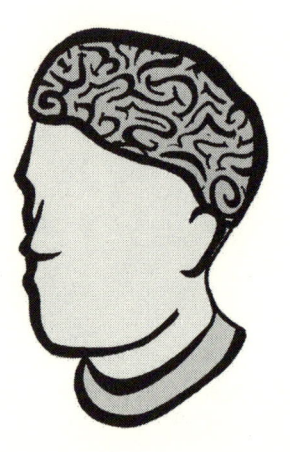

= BEE BA DO DUM DUM, BUM BADUM BUM BUH, BAH DUH, BAH DAH DUM DUM, DUM DEDUM DUM DUM DUM DUM. BADA DO DUM DEDUM. =

Soloveitchik notes that Jewish tradition has always been transmitted in two ways: mimesis and texts. After times of hardship, it is common for the mimesis to be written down and turned into text because of the instinct to retreat in times of hardship that Rabbi Adler described above. Soloveitchik laments the transition from experience based learning to text, believing the mimesis to be the vital part of the tradition. On Seder night, experience's primacy is evermore true. We cannot just sit around the apartment and talk about our history, we must live it too. *Seinfeld* would have needed a lot more sets to film if Jerry, George, Elaine, and Kramer believed that too.

The Forced "I Love You"

Anoose, usually translated as "coerced," is a strange way to describe why Jacob and his family traveled to Egypt. They weren't actually forced. They could have theoretically stayed in Canaan even if Joseph was in Egypt. No one ever forced them to go to Egypt. In this context "coerced by Divine decree" is even more vexing, considering God never actually commands Jacob he must go down. Rabbi Yosef Dov Solevetichik notes that God did indeed force Jacob to go down to Egypt because He created a situation where there was only one reasonable course of action. Due to the famine and the new

וַיֵּרֶד מִצְרַיְמָה — אָנוּס עַל פִּי הַדִּבּוּר.

בִּי בַּה דוּ דוֹם דוֹם, בּוֹם בַּדוּם בּוֹם בֹּן, בַּה דוּי, בַּה דֵּה דוּם דוֹם, דוֹם דַדוּם דוֹם דוֹם דוֹם. בַּדֵה דוּ דוֹם דַדוֹם.

knowledge that his son Joseph was alive there left Jacob with only one real option. His choice can then be seen as by "Divine decree."

Having no other practical choice is also how being forced is defined in Seinfeld. In "The Ex-Girlfriend[C99]," George feels compelled to say "I love you" to his girlfriend. He and Jerry have the following interchange:

> GEORGE: Oh, I had no choice. She squeezed it out of me! She'd tell me she loved me. Alright, at first, I just look at her. I'd go "Oh, really?" or "Boy, that's, that's something." But, eventually you have to come back with "Well, I love you." You know, you can only hold out for so long!
> JERRY: You're a human being.
> GEORGE: And I didn't even ask her out. She asked me out first. She called me up. What was I supposed to do? Say no? I can't do that to someone.
> JERRY: You're too nice a guy.
> GEORGE: I am. I'm a nice guy... (realizing) And she seduced me! We were in my apartment, I'm sitting on the couch, she's on the chair — I get up to go to the bathroom, I come back, she's on the couch. What am I supposed to do? Not do anything? I couldn't do that. I would've insulted her.
> JERRY: You're flesh and blood.

Twice George feels "forced" not because he actually was forced, but because the situation largely demanded one course of action. He felt forced to say "I love you" not because she actually required him to but because the situation only allowed for one option. Similarly, the physical relationship started because he felt "forced" in the same way.

In "The Pez Dispenser[C100]," George feels forced to listen to Noel, his girlfriend, because he has no power in the relationship. He is on a quest to not feel coerced in the relationship, not because she actually forces him, but because she has all the "hand." He tells Jerry: "I have no hand — no hand at all. She has the hand; I have *no* hand..." Noel has all the implicit power in the relationship, and this circumstance is tantamount to George feeling coerced. To George, as well as to Rav Soloveitchik, having no hand is as good as being forced.

"And he resided there" — this teaches that Yaakov, our father, didn't go down to settle in Egypt, but rather to only reside there, as it is stated (Genesis 47:4), "And they said to Pharaoh, 'To reside in the land have we come, since there is not enough pasture for your servant's flocks, since the famine is heavy in the land of Canaan, and now please grant that your servants should dwell in the Land of Goshen.'"

"As a small number" — as it is stated (Deuteronomy 10:22), "With seventy souls did your ancestors come down to Egypt, and now the Lord your God has made you as numerous as the stars of the sky and the amount of gum Lloyd Braun bought Jerry[39]."

═ BEE BA DO DUM DUM, BUM BADUM BUM BUH, BAH DUH, BAH DAH DUM DUM, DUM DEDUM DUM DUM DUM DUM. BADA DO DUM DEDUM. ═

The Key Visitors

In "The Keys[C101]," Kramer realizes has been overstaying his welcome in Jerry's apartment. He uses the spare keys Jerry gave him in a variety of inappropriate situations such as: using his bath, going in late at night for food, or spending romantic time with his girlfriend, generally breaking the "covenant of the keys." Jerry therefore decides to take his keys back which puts Kramer in a tailspin. He no longer acts like himself especially around Jerry. Kramer explains why to George:

Because you see, George, having the keys to Jerry's apartment? That kept me in a fantasy world. Every time I went over to his house, it was like I was on vacation. Better food, better view, better TV. And cleaner? Oh - much cleaner. That became my reality. I ignored the squalor in my own life because I'm looking at life, you see, through Jerry's eyes.

Kramer realizes that his visits to Jerry's apartment affected him. He goes and cannot shake the ultimately false atmosphere of Jerry's comparative luxury. Similarly, in "The Chicken Roaster[C102]," Jerry and Kramer switch apartments because there is a neon sign with a red blinking light going into Kramer's apartment and Jerry is a much

THE (UNOFFICIAL) SEINFELD HAGGADAH

וַיָּגָר שָׁם — מְלַמֵּד שֶׁלֹּא יָרַד יַעֲקֹב אָבִינוּ לְהִשְׁתַּקֵּעַ בְּמִצְרַיִם אֶלָּא לָגוּר שָׁם, שֶׁנֶּאֱמַר (בראשית מז, ד): "וַיֹּאמְרוּ אֶל־פַּרְעֹה, 'לָגוּר בָּאָרֶץ בָּאנוּ, כִּי אֵין מִרְעֶה לַצֹּאן אֲשֶׁר לַעֲבָדֶיךָ, כִּי כָבֵד הָרָעָב בְּאֶרֶץ כְּנָעַן. וְעַתָּה יֵשְׁבוּ־נָא עֲבָדֶיךָ בְּאֶרֶץ גֹּשֶׁן.'"

בִּמְתֵי מְעָט — כְּמָה שֶׁנֶּאֱמַר (דברים י, כב): "בְּשִׁבְעִים נֶפֶשׁ יָרְדוּ אֲבֹתֶיךָ מִצְרָיְמָה, וְעַתָּה שָׂמְךָ ה' אֱלֹהֶיךָ כְּכוֹכְבֵי הַשָּׁמַיִם לָרֹב."

בי בה דו דום דום, בום בדום בום בו, בה דו, בה דה דום דום, דום דדום דום דום דום. בדה דו דום דדום.

deeper sleeper. This switch has a bigger effect than they realize. Jerry begins acting like Kramer. He hatches schemes, befriends Bob Sacamano, and takes on Kramer's general mannerisms. He even uses his catch phrases like "Giddy Up." Jerry "turns into" Kramer from residing in his apartment for a time.

What happened to Kramer with the keys and to Jerry in Kramer's apartment happens to the Jewish people "visiting" Egypt. They only went to reside there and not to settle. Jacob does not understand the effect residing will have on his descendants. They only go down because of the famine, but quickly residing turns into settling. The Midrash describes how the Jewish people largely turned into Egyptians, and were only able to keep their dress, names and language. All three situations show how hard it is to keep your identity when being in a land that is not your own, and all three only learn the lesson when the situation has reconciled: Kramer when he gets the keys back, Jerry when he gets back his apartment, and the Jewish people when they are eventually saved in the story we read now.

מגיד — 67

"And they became a nation there" — this teaches that Israel developed their distinctive ways there. Not that there's anything wrong with that[40].

"Great, powerful" — as it is stated (Exodus 1:7), "And the Children of Israel were fruitful and increased abundantly and multiplied and grew exceedingly mighty, and the land was filled with them."

"And numerous" — as it is stated (Ezekiel 16:7), "I have given you to be numerous as the vegetation of a big salad[41], and you increased and grew and became highly ornamented, your breasts were set, real, and spectacular[42], and your hair grew with flowing locks that you could still get your fingers out of it[43], but you were bad naked[44] and barren. And when I passed by you and saw you wallowing in your fridge full of blood[45], I said to you, 'by your blood you shall live.' I said to you, 'by your blood you shall live.'"

═ BEE BA DO DUM DUM, BUM BADUM BUM BUH, BAH DUH, BAH DAH DUM DUM, DUM DEDUM DUM DUM DUM DUM. BADA DO DUM DEDUM. ═

The Blood Brothers

What blood is Ezekiel talking about? By what blood should we live? Shemot Rabba, a set of Rabbinic teachings on Exodus, gives a twofold answer: this blood is the blood of the Paschal sacrifice and the blood of circumcision. What does this Midrash imply?

In "The Blood[C103]," after Jerry gets injured by a knife he gets a blood transfusion from Kramer's blood, which Kramer has been hoarding in his own freezer. Kramer describes them now being "blood brothers" because they share the same blood now. Jerry is prescient on what this means as he says: "I can feel his blood inside of me. Borrowing things from my blood." Kramer indeed goes on to use the fact that they are blood brothers to get further favors from Jerry.

THE (UNOFFICIAL) SEINFELD HAGGADAH

וַיְהִי שָׁם לְגוֹי — מְלַמֵד שֶׁהָיוּ יִשְׂרָאֵל מְצֻיָּנִים שָׁם.

גָּדוֹל עָצוּם — כְּמָה שֶׁנֶּאֱמַר (שמות א, ז): "וּבְנֵי יִשְׂרָאֵל פָּרוּ וַיִּשְׁרְצוּ וַיִּרְבּוּ וַיַּעַצְמוּ בִּמְאֹד מְאֹד, וַתִּמָּלֵא הָאָרֶץ אֹתָם."

וָרָב — כְּמָה שֶׁנֶּאֱמַר (יחזקאל טז, ז): "רְבָבָה כְּצֶמַח הַשָּׂדֶה נְתַתִּיךְ, וַתִּרְבִּי וַתִּגְדְּלִי וַתָּבֹאִי בַּעֲדִי עֲדָיִים, שָׁדַיִם נָכֹנוּ וּשְׂעָרֵךְ צִמֵּחַ, וְאַתְּ עֵרֹם וְעֶרְיָה. וָאֶעֱבֹר עָלַיִךְ וָאֶרְאֵךְ מִתְבּוֹסֶסֶת בְּדָמָיִךְ, וָאֹמַר לָךְ 'בְּדָמַיִךְ חֲיִי, וָאֹמַר לָךְ בְּדָמַיִךְ חֲיִי.'"

בִּי בַה דוּ דוֹם דוֹם, בּוֹם בַדוֹם בּוֹם בֹּו, בַה דוּ, בַה דַח דוּם דוֹם, דוֹם דַדוֹם דוֹם דוֹם דוֹם דוֹם. בַדַה דוּ דוֹם דַדוּם.

The Jewish people are all blood siblings. The Paschal sacrifice consecrates this and circumcision continues it. During the Exodus, we were becoming a nation and we were required to use the blood from the sacrifice to put on our doorways. Through this collective use of blood we became blood brothers and sisters. We continue this tradition to this day declaring that we are all one nation, even if we shouldnt always expect the insane favors Kramer does.

"And the Egyptians did bad to us, and afflicted us, and put upon us hard work" (Deuteronomy 26:6).

"**And the Egyptians did bad to us**" — as it is stated (Exodus 1:10), "Let us be phony[46] with them, lest they multiply and it will be that when war is called, they too will join with our enemies and fight against us and go up from the land."

"**And afflicted us**" — as it is stated (Exodus 1:11); "And they placed upon them taxmasters to afflict them with their burdens; and they built storage cities, Pithom and Raamses," and pushed around Rickshaws[47].

"**And put upon us hard work**" — as it is stated (Exodus 1:11), "And they enslaved the children of Israel with back breaking work." Even though they didn't even work there[48]!

"**And we cried out to the Lord, the God of our ancestors, and the Lord heard our voice, and He looked upon our affliction, and our toil and our duress**" (Deuteronomy 26:7).

═ BEE BA DO DUM DUM, BUM BADUM BUM BUH, BAH DUH, BAH DAH DUM DUM, DUM DEDUM DUM DUM DUM DUM. BADA DO DUM DEDUM. ═

The Crying Out

Why did the Jewish people finally decide to cry out? The Ohr Hachaim, the 18th century Moroccan Biblical commentary, states that:

> They did not appeal to God to save them from their situation; they merely groaned, something which people who feel that their burdens are too great are wont to do out of a sense of helplessness. The Torah informs us that although this outcry was not a direct appeal to God for help, it did reach the ears of God because their situation was indeed intolerable; this is why the Torah adds that the reason God responded was "from the work."

THE (UNOFFICIAL) SEINFELD HAGGADAH

"וַיָּרֵעוּ אֹתָנוּ הַמִּצְרִים וַיְעַנּוּנוּ, וַיִּתְּנוּ עָלֵינוּ עֲבֹדָה קָשָׁה" (דברים כו, ו).

וַיָּרֵעוּ אֹתָנוּ הַמִּצְרִים — כְּמָה שֶׁנֶּאֱמַר (שמות א, י): "הָבָה נִתְחַכְּמָה לוֹ פֶּן יִרְבֶּה, וְהָיָה כִּי תִקְרֶאנָה מִלְחָמָה וְנוֹסַף גַּם הוּא עַל שֹׂנְאֵינוּ וְנִלְחַם־בָּנוּ, וְעָלָה מִן־הָאָרֶץ."

וַיְעַנּוּנוּ — כְּמָה שֶׁנֶּאֱמַר (שמות א, יא): "וַיָּשִׂימוּ עָלָיו שָׂרֵי מִסִּים לְמַעַן עַנֹּתוֹ בְּסִבְלֹתָם. וַיִּבֶן עָרֵי מִסְכְּנוֹת לְפַרְעֹה. אֶת־פִּתֹם וְאֶת־רַעַמְסֵס."

וַיִּתְּנוּ עָלֵינוּ עֲבֹדָה קָשָׁה — כְּמָה שֶׁנֶּאֱמַר (שמות א, יא): "וַיַּעֲבִדוּ מִצְרַיִם אֶת־בְּנֵי יִשְׂרָאֵל בְּפָרֶךְ."

"וַנִּצְעַק אֶל־ה' אֱלֹהֵי אֲבֹתֵינוּ, וַיִּשְׁמַע ה' אֶת־קֹלֵנוּ, וַיַּרְא אֶת־עָנְיֵנוּ וְאֶת עֲמָלֵנוּ וְאֶת לַחֲצֵנוּ" (דברים כו, ז).

SERENITY NOW!

מגיד — 71

"And we cried out to the Lord, the God of our ancestors" — as it is stated (Exodus 2:23); "And it was in those many days that the king of Egypt died and the Children of Israel sighed from the work and yelled out 'SERENITY NOW!'[49], and their supplication went up to God from the work."

"And the Lord heard our voice" — as it is stated (Exodus 2:24); "And God heard their groans (Hellooooooo[50]) and God remembered His covenant with Avraham and with Yitzchak and with Yaakov."

═ BEE BA DO DUM DUM, BUM BADUM BUM BUH, BAH DUH, BAH DAH DUM DUM, DUM DEDUM DUM DUM DUM DUM. BADA DO DUM DEDUM. ═

They cried out not to God, but in hopelessness, and in that moment of true need God hears them.

In "The Fix Up[C104]," George makes a similar point when discussing his dating life:

> GEORGE: I don't want hope. Hope is killing me. My dream is to become hopeless. When you're hopeless, you don't care, and when you don't care, that indifference makes you attractive.
> JERRY: Oh, so hopelessness is the key.
> GEORGE: It's my only hope.

The philosophy that being hopeless makes you more attractive plays out in the Exodus story. God sees how hopeless the Jewish people are and wants to fulfill the promise made to Abraham, Isaac, and Jacob. The people were so busy with their work that there was no real hope for them as a nation. It is at that point of despair, and no later, when they needed to be taken out of Egypt. The people had become hopeless, and God saw their quota was at the max already.

The Amaleinu

The worst type of work is not work that is hard, but work that is meaningless. The Talmud (Sota 11a) describes the toil of the Egyptians, "amaleinu," as working without purpose at all. The Egyptians gave

THE (UNOFFICIAL) SEINFELD HAGGADAH

וַנִּצְעַק אֶל־ה' אֱלֹהֵי אֲבֹתֵינוּ — כְּמָה שֶׁנֶּאֱמַר (שמות ב, כג): "וַיְהִי בַיָּמִים הָרַבִּים הָהֵם וַיָּמָת מֶלֶךְ מִצְרַיִם, וַיֵּאָנְחוּ בְנֵי־יִשְׂרָאֵל מִן־הָעֲבוֹדָה וַיִּזְעָקוּ, וַתַּעַל שַׁוְעָתָם אֶל־הָאֱלֹהִים מִן הָעֲבֹדָה."

וַיִּשְׁמַע ה' אֶת קֹלֵנוּ — כְּמָה שֶׁנֶּאֱמַר (שמות ב, כד): "וַיִּשְׁמַע אֱלֹהִים אֶת־נַאֲקָתָם, וַיִּזְכֹּר אֱלֹהִים אֶת־בְּרִיתוֹ אֶת־אַבְרָהָם, אֶת־יִצְחָק וְאֶת־יַעֲקֹב."

―――― בִּי בָּה דוּ דוּם דוּם, בּוּם בְּדוּם בּוּם בּוֹ, בָּה דוּ, בָּה דָּה דוּם דוּם, דוּם דְּדוּם דוּם דוּם דוּם דוּם. בָּדָה דוּ דוּם דְּדוּם, ――――

the Jews jobs that were not only extremely hard, but pointless in nature. While working for Mr. Pitt, Elaine seems to be undergoing a lot of amaleinu. She has meaningless tasks like taking all the salt off of his pretzels[C105], and getting him socks[C106] that fit exactly the way he wants. There are many jobs that are "bad," but this type of job is the worst (even if it isn't backbreaking). Thankfully, Mr. Pitt is not doing this purposely to Elaine and she has the power to leave. The work isn't completely meaningless because she still is getting paid. And yet still, Elaine can't wait to leave. The Jews in Egypt enjoyed none of those options, making their work true toil.

מגיד — 73

"And He looked upon our affliction" — this refers to the separation between husband and wife, as it is stated (Exodus 2:25); "And God saw the Children of Israel and God knew."

"And our toil" — this refers to the killing of the sons, as it is stated (Exodus 1:24); "Every boy that is born, throw him into the Nile and every girl you shall keep alive."

"And our duress" — this refers to the force used, as it is stated (Exodus 3:9); "And I also saw the duress that the Egyptians are applying on them."

"And the Lord took us out of Egypt with a mighty hand and with an outstretched arm, and with great awe, and with signs, and with wonders" (Deuteronomy 26:8).

"And the Lord took us out of Egypt" — not through an angel and not through a seraph and not through a messenger, but directly by the Holy One, blessed be He, Himself, as it is stated (Exodus 12:12); "And I will pass through the Land of Egypt on that night and I will smite every firstborn in the Land of Egypt, from men to animals; and with all the gods of Egypt, I will make judgments, I am the Lord."
  "And I will pass through the Land of Egypt" — I, and not an angel.
  "And I will smite every firstborn" — I, and not a seraph. Or any mannequin that looks like it[51].
  "And with all the gods of Egypt, I will make judgments" — I, and not a messenger.
  "I am the Lord" — I am He, and there is no other.

THE (UNOFFICIAL) SEINFELD HAGGADAH

וַיַּרְא אֶת־עָנְיֵנוּ — זוֹ פְּרִישׁוּת דֶּרֶךְ אֶרֶץ, כְּמָה שֶׁנֶּאֱמַר (שמות ב, כה): "וַיַּרְא אֱלֹהִים אֶת בְּנֵי־יִשְׂרָאֵל וַיֵּדַע אֱלֹהִים."

וְאֶת־עֲמָלֵנוּ — אֵלּוּ הַבָּנִים. כְּמָה שֶׁנֶּאֱמַר (שמות א, כד): "כָּל־הַבֵּן הַיִּלּוֹד הַיְאֹרָה תַּשְׁלִיכֻהוּ וְכָל־הַבַּת תְּחַיּוּן."

וְאֶת לַחֲצֵנוּ — זֶה הַדְּחָק, כְּמָה שֶׁנֶּאֱמַר (שמות ג, ט): "וְגַם־רָאִיתִי אֶת־הַלַּחַץ אֲשֶׁר מִצְרַיִם לֹחֲצִים אֹתָם."

וַיּוֹצִאֵנוּ ה' מִמִּצְרַיִם בְּיָד חֲזָקָה, וּבִזְרֹעַ נְטוּיָה, וּבְמֹרָא גָּדֹל, וּבְאֹתוֹת וּבְמֹפְתִים" (דברים כו, ח).

וַיּוֹצִאֵנוּ ה' מִמִּצְרַיִם — לֹא עַל־יְדֵי מַלְאָךְ, וְלֹא עַל־יְדֵי שָׂרָף, וְלֹא עַל־יְדֵי שָׁלִיחַ, אֶלָּא הַקָּדוֹשׁ בָּרוּךְ הוּא בִּכְבוֹדוֹ וּבְעַצְמוֹ. שֶׁנֶּאֱמַר: "וְעָבַרְתִּי בְאֶרֶץ מִצְרַיִם בַּלַּיְלָה הַזֶּה, וְהִכֵּיתִי כָל־בְּכוֹר בְּאֶרֶץ מִצְרַיִם מֵאָדָם וְעַד בְּהֵמָה, וּבְכָל אֱלֹהֵי מִצְרַיִם אֶעֱשֶׂה שְׁפָטִים. אֲנִי ה'."

וְעָבַרְתִּי בְאֶרֶץ מִצְרַיִם בַּלַּיְלָה הַזֶּה — אֲנִי וְלֹא מַלְאָךְ.

וְהִכֵּיתִי כָל בְּכוֹר בְּאֶרֶץ־מִצְרַיִם — אֲנִי וְלֹא שָׂרָף.

וּבְכָל־אֱלֹהֵי מִצְרַיִם אֶעֱשֶׂה שְׁפָטִים — אֲנִי וְלֹא הַשָּׁלִיחַ.

אֲנִי ה' — אֲנִי הוּא וְלֹא אַחֵר.

מגיד — 75

"**With a mighty hand**" — this refers to the pestilence, as it is stated (Exodus 9:3); "Behold the hand of the Lord is upon your herds that are in the field, upon the horses, upon the donkeys, upon the camels, upon the cattle and upon the flocks, there will be a very heavy pestilence." Unlike George's pretty hands which are what comes from avoiding manual labor your whole life[52].

"**And with an outstretched arm**" — this refers to the sword, as it is stated (I Chronicles 21:16), "And His sword was drawn in His hand, leaning over Jerusalem."

"**And with great awe**" — this refers to the revelation of the Divine Presence, as it is stated (Deuteronomy 4:34), "Or did God try to take for Himself a nation from within a nation with enigmas, with signs and with wonders and with war and with a strong hand and with an outstretched forearm and with great and awesome acts, according to all that the Lord, your God, did for you in Egypt in front of your eyes?"

"**And with signs**" — this refers to the staff, as it is stated (Exodus 4:17), "And this staff you shall take in your hand, that with it you will perform signs."

"**And with wonders**" — this refers to the blood, as it is stated (Joel 3:3); "And I will place my wonders in the skies and in the earth."

בְּיָד חֲזָקָה – זוֹ הַדֶּבֶר, כְּמָה שֶׁנֶּאֱמַר (שמות ט, ג): "הִנֵּה יַד־ה' הוֹיָה בְּמִקְנְךָ אֲשֶׁר בַּשָּׂדֶה, בַּסּוּסִים, בַּחֲמֹרִים, בַּגְּמַלִּים, בַּבָּקָר וּבַצֹּאן, דֶּבֶר כָּבֵד מְאֹד."

וּבִזְרֹעַ נְטוּיָה – זוֹ הַחֶרֶב, כְּמָה שֶׁנֶּאֱמַר (דברי הימים א' כא, טז): "וְחַרְבּוֹ שְׁלוּפָה בְּיָדוֹ, נְטוּיָה עַל־יְרוּשָׁלָיִם."

וּבְמוֹרָא גָּדֹל – זוֹ גִּלּוּי שְׁכִינָה. כְּמָה שֶׁנֶּאֱמַר (דברים ד, לד): "אוֹ הֲנִסָּה אֱלֹהִים לָבוֹא לָקַחַת לוֹ גוֹי מִקֶּרֶב גּוֹי בְּמַסֹּת בְּאֹתֹת וּבְמוֹפְתִים וּבְמִלְחָמָה וּבְיָד חֲזָקָה וּבִזְרוֹעַ נְטוּיָה וּבְמוֹרָאִים גְּדֹלִים כְּכֹל אֲשֶׁר־עָשָׂה לָכֶם ה' אֱלֹהֵיכֶם בְּמִצְרַיִם לְעֵינֶיךָ."

וּבְאֹתוֹת – זֶה הַמַּטֶּה, כְּמָה שֶׁנֶּאֱמַר (שמות ד, יז): "וְאֶת הַמַּטֶּה הַזֶּה תִּקַּח בְּיָדְךָ, אֲשֶׁר תַּעֲשֶׂה־בּוֹ אֶת הָאֹתֹת."

וּבְמוֹפְתִים – זֶה הַדָּם, כְּמָה שֶׁנֶּאֱמַר (יואל ג, ג): "וְנָתַתִּי מוֹפְתִים בַּשָּׁמַיִם וּבָאָרֶץ."

THE TEN PLAGUES

When we say "blood and fire and pillars of smoke" and the ten plagues and "detsakh," "adash" and "be'achab," we pour out a little wine from our cup, usually with our pinky finger. Just make sure the napkin that the drop of wine goes onto isn't cashmere. The red dot might not come out[53].

"Blood and Fire and Pillars of smoke."

═ BEE BA DO DUM DUM, BUM BADUM BUM BUH, BAH DUH, BAH DAH DUM DUM, DUM DEDUM DUM DUM DUM DUM. BADA DO DUM DEDUM. ═

The Schadenfreude

Our *Seinfeld* characters don't seem too distressed when other people have problems. The most classic example of this is one of Jerry's catch phrases, "that's a shame." Jerry is consistently nonplussed when others fall on their faces, sometimes literally. In "The Boyfriend[C107]," George needs Jerry to answer the phone for the unemployment office pretending to be an employer who interviewed George for a position as a latex salesman. While George is in the bathroom, Kramer answers the phone not knowing the ruse, and tells the unemployment clerk that they have the wrong number. George, in an effort to tell Kramer, runs out of the bathroom with his pants at his ankles, and falls on his face. Instead of being upset for George, Jerry's response is: "and you want to be my latex salesman?" Similarly, in "The Stock Tip[C108]," Kramer is excited when George and Jerry's investment fails.

In "The Gum[C109]," George is happy when his childhood "nemesis" Lloyd Braun needs to get help in a mental institution. George and a childhood neighbor Deena have the following conversation:

> GEORGE: I'm not the one with the problem. Lloyd Braun was in the nuthouse, not me.
> DEENA: Yet again, taking pleasure in the misfortunes of others.
> GEORGE: All my friends do that.

As a group, they are especially happy when it affects them positively. Most glaringly, George confuses the doctor when he seems somewhat relieved when the doctor tells him his fiance, Susan, passed away, since he was trying to find a way to break off the

עשרת המכות

When we say "blood and fire and pillars of smoke" and the ten plagues and "detsakh," "adash" and "be'achab," we pour out a little wine from our cup, usually with our pinky finger. Just make sure the napkin that the drop of wine goes onto isn't cashmere. The red dot might not come out.

"דָּם וָאֵשׁ וְתִימְרוֹת עָשָׁן."

Reinfeld

בי בה דו דום דום, בום בדום בום בו, בה דו, בה דה דום דום, דום דדום דום דום דום דום, בדה דו דום דדום.

relationship[C110]. In "The Trip: Part 2[C111]," Kramer, George, and Jerry are happy that another murder took place because it exonerated Kramer. In "The Soup Nazi[C112]," George is happy Jerry broke up with his girlfriend because their public displays of affection annoy him. In "The Baby Shower[C113]," Elaine is gleeful that an old date bumps into Jerry at the party and is furious at him for not calling her back. In all these situations and more, our four "heroes" are happy at others misfortune.

Even in the thick of learning about the Exodus, and how abominable the Egyptians were to us, we are not encouraged to embrace the *Seinfeld* characters' level of schadenfreude. Rav Samson Raphael Hirsch, the 19th century German philosopher, is quoted as understanding that instead of rejoicing in the demise of the Egyptians, and the plagues that befell them, we mourn by taking a little wine out of our cup (many dip a finger in to take some out). Similarly, one explanation for not saying full Hallel on the last days of Pesach is that we are not fully celebrating the destruction of the Egyptians during the splitting of the sea. We actualize Proverbs 24:17 at the Seder which says "When your enemy falls, you shall not rejoice."

THE HAGGADAH ABOUT NOTHING

Another explanation: "With a strong hand," two words correspond to two plagues; "and with an outstretched forearm," two words correspond to two plagues; "and with great awe," two words correspond to two plagues; "and with signs," plural corresponds to two plagues; "and with wonders," plural corresponds to two plagues.

These are the ten plagues that the Holy One, blessed be He, brought on the Egyptians in Egypt and they are:

(Parentheses refer to what the plague might have looked like in the Seinfeld universe)

Blood (all wine turns into pepsi[54])
Frogs (high score games battery running out[55])
Lice (I have fleas![56])
Flies (All cars become smelly[57])
Pestilence (having the Kavorka[58])
Boils (People develop goiters[59])
Hail (Junior Mints falling from sky[60])
Locusts (Lupus? is it Lupus?[61])
Darkness (Stuck in Parking Garage for 3 days[62])
Killing of the Firstborn
(Forced to lick poisonous envelopes[63])

Rabbi Yehuda used to abbreviate the plagues with mnemonics:

De'tsakh [the Hebrew initials of the first three plagues],
A'dash [the Hebrew initials of the second three plagues],
Be'achav [the Hebrew initials of the last four plagues].

THE (UNOFFICIAL) SEINFELD HAGGADAH

דָּבָר אַחֵר: "בְּיָד חֲזָקָה" שְׁתַּיִם, "וּבִזְרֹעַ נְטוּיָה" שְׁתַּיִם, "וּבְמֹרָא גָּדֹל" - שְׁתַּיִם, "וּבְאֹתוֹת" - שְׁתַּיִם, "וּבְמֹפְתִים" - שְׁתַּיִם.

אֵלּוּ עֶשֶׂר מַכּוֹת שֶׁהֵבִיא הַקָּדוֹשׁ בָּרוּךְ הוּא עַל־הַמִּצְרִים בְּמִצְרַיִם, וְאֵלּוּ הֵן:

דָּם, צְפַרְדֵּעַ, כִּנִּים, עָרוֹב, דֶּבֶר, שְׁחִין, בָּרָד, אַרְבֶּה, חֹשֶׁךְ, מַכַּת בְּכוֹרוֹת.

רַבִּי יְהוּדָה הָיָה נוֹתֵן בָּהֶם סִמָּנִים:
דְּצַ"ךְ
עֲדַ"שׁ
בְּאַחַ"ב.

בִּי בַּה דוּ דוּם דוּם, בּוּם בַּדוּם בּוּם בּוּ, בַּה דוּ, בַּה דַה דוּם דוּם, דוּם דַדוּם דוּם דוּם דוּם. בַּדַה דוּ דוּם דוּם.

The Mnemonics

A lot of minor *Seinfeld* characters have odd quirks, and Jerry doesn't shy away from the quirks when discussing these acquaintances. These people include: the close talker[C114] (a person who gets too close when he talks to you), the high talker[C115] (a guy who's tone is very high that he sounds like a woman), the sidler[C116] (Elaine's coworker who gets right next to you without hearing them), or the soup nazi[C117] (see the dvar Torah about singing the seder order) to name a few. The name that Jerry gives the character always seems

מגיד — 81

to be vital in the story. The nickname makes it easy for the gang to understand, nevermind we the audience.

What Jerry does is similar to what Rebbi Yehuda does at the Seder. He combines the plagues into three groups and gives a mnemonic for them. Rebbi Yehuda is actually known for doing this, and has other mnemonics in the Gemara. The explanation for doing so may be based on his statement in the Sifri, a collection of Rabbinic teachings, (Devarim 32:2) where it says: "A person should always organize his Torah thoughts by general topic for if one just gathers

═ BEE BA DO DUM DUM, BUM BADUM BUM BUH, BAH DUH, BAH DAH DUM DUM, DUM DEDUM DUM DUM DUM DUM. BADA DO DUM DEDUM. ═

Rabbi Yose Hagelili says, "From where can you derive that the Egyptians were struck with ten plagues in Egypt and were then struck with fifty plagues at the Sea? In Egypt, what does it state? 'Then the magicians said unto Pharaoh: "This is the finger of God"' (We need not follow the car with Danny Tartabull[64]) (Exodus 8:15). And at the sea, what does it state? 'And Israel saw the Lord's great hand that he used upon the Egyptians, and the people feared the Lord; and they believed

═ BEE BA DO DUM DUM, BUM BADUM BUM BUH, BAH DUH, BAH DAH DUM DUM, DUM DEDUM DUM DUM DUM DUM. BADA DO DUM DEDUM. ═

The Grateful Math

This part of the Haggadah is really odd (perhaps even?). There is a list of Rabbis counting the number of plagues brought on the Egyptians, and each Rabbi cites a higher amount. Rabbi Hayyim Angel, Professor of Bible at Yeshiva University, notes that these texts borrow language from Psalms, specifically 78 and 106. Both of these Psalms talk about how ungrateful the Jewish people were and how we should learn to be grateful. In this context, the Haggadah is trying to rectify past ungratefulness by overcompensating in expressing gratitude. These Rabbis commemorate what was done for us by consistently upping the stakes of how much we should be thankful. Rabbi Lord Jonathan Sacks, former chief Rabbi of the UK, says something similar about Dayenu:

> "This (Dayenu) song is a tikkun, a making-right, for the ingratitude of the Israelites in the wilderness. At almost every stage of the way they

THE (UNOFFICIAL) SEINFELD HAGGADAH

details they will be overwhelmed, and will not know what to do." The meaning of the mnemonic is dealt with in many Haggadahs, but, more generally, Rabbi Yehuda seems to be doing something similar to Jerry. Jerry is organizing people based on their unique qualities to make life more understandable to his friends by proxy for the audience. Rabbi Yehuda expands that concept to the Exodus story, and to everything else. When reminiscing on the way Hashem took us out, we need not get lost in all the details, but use the details to further our understanding of the bigger ideas.

===== בי בה דו דום דום, בום בדום בום בו, בה די, בה דה דום דום, דום דדום דום דום דום דום. בדה דו דום דדום. =====

רַבִּי יוֹסֵי הַגְּלִילִי אוֹמֵר: "מִנַּיִן אַתָּה אוֹמֵר שֶׁלָּקוּ הַמִּצְרִים בְּמִצְרַיִם עֶשֶׂר מַכּוֹת וְעַל הַיָּם לָקוּ חֲמִשִּׁים מַכּוֹת? בְּמִצְרַיִם מָה הוּא אוֹמֵר? 'וַיֹּאמְרוּ הַחַרְטֻמִּם אֶל פַּרְעֹה: "אֶצְבַּע אֱלֹהִים הִוא"' (שמות ח, טו), וְעַל הַיָּם מָה הוּא אוֹמֵר? 'וַיַּרְא יִשְׂרָאֵל אֶת־הַיָּד הַגְּדֹלָה אֲשֶׁר עָשָׂה ה' בְּמִצְרַיִם, וַיִּירְאוּ הָעָם אֶת־ה', וַיַּאֲמִינוּ בַּה' וּבְמֹשֶׁה עַבְדּוֹ' (שמות יד, לא). כַּמָּה לָקוּ בְאֶצְבַּע? עֶשֶׂר מַכּוֹת. אֱמוֹר מֵעַתָּה: בְּמִצְרַיִם לָקוּ עֶשֶׂר מַכּוֹת וְעַל הַיָּם לָקוּ חֲמִשִּׁים מַכּוֹת."

The sea was angry that day, my friends.

in the Lord, and in Moshe, His servant' (Exodus 14:31). How many were they struck with the finger? Ten plagues. You can say from here that in Egypt, they were struck with ten plagues and at the sea, they were struck with fifty plagues."

Rabbi Eliezer says, "From where can you derive that every plague that the Holy One, blessed be He, brought upon the Egyptians in Egypt was composed of four plagues? As it is stated (Psalms 78:49): 'He sent upon them the fierceness of His anger, wrath, and fury, and trouble, a sending of messengers of evil.' 'Wrath' corresponds to one; 'and fury' brings it to two; 'and trouble' brings it to three; 'a sending of messengers of evil' brings it to four. You can deduce from here that in Egypt, they were struck with forty plagues and at the Sea, they were struck with two hundred plagues."

═══ BEE BA DO DUM DUM, BUM BADUM BUM BUH, BAH DUH, BAH DAH DUM DUM, DUM DEDUM DUM DUM DUM DUM. BADA DO DUM DEDUM. ═══

> complained: about the water, food, the difficulties of the journey, the challenge of conquering the land. It is as if the poet is saying: Where they complained, let us give thanks. Each stage was a miracle. As Hegel points out, slavery gives rise to a culture of ressentment, a generalized discontent; and the Israelites were newly freed slaves. One of the signs of freedom is the capacity for gratitude."

Having been slaves in Egypt, we lost our ability to give thanks, at the Seder, we reclaim it in an over the top fashion.

Like how the Psalms describe the Jews leaving Egypt, Jerry is not an especially thankful person. In "The Face Painter[C118]," Alec Berg gives Jerry and Kramer tickets to a Rangers playoff game. Jerry doesn't want to thank Alec after the game because he believes he is "taking a stand against all this overthanking." Kramer eventually gets him to call after much prodding, but it's too late. They are going to the game, but only if they sit in the nosebleeds and paint their chests. Similarly, in "The Soup[C119]," Banya, a fellow comedian who Jerry openly disdains, gifts him an Armani suit. Jerry is not very grateful for the suit. When Banya asks him to just take him out to dinner for

THE (UNOFFICIAL) SEINFELD HAGGADAH

רַבִּי אֱלִיעֶזֶר אוֹמֵר: "מִנַּיִן שֶׁכָּל־מַכָּה וּמַכָּה שֶׁהֵבִיא הַקָּדוֹשׁ בָּרוּךְ הוּא עַל הַמִּצְרִים בְּמִצְרַיִם הָיְתָה שֶׁל אַרְבַּע מַכּוֹת? שֶׁנֶּאֱמַר (תהלים עח, מט): 'יְשַׁלַּח־בָּם חֲרוֹן אַפּוֹ, עֶבְרָה וָזַעַם וְצָרָה, מִשְׁלַחַת מַלְאֲכֵי רָעִים.' 'עֶבְרָה' – אַחַת, 'וָזַעַם' – שְׁתַּיִם, 'וְצָרָה' – שָׁלֹשׁ, 'מִשְׁלַחַת מַלְאֲכֵי רָעִים' – אַרְבַּע. אֱמוֹר מֵעַתָּה: בְּמִצְרַיִם לָקוּ אַרְבָּעִים מַכּוֹת וְעַל הַיָּם לָקוּ מָאתַיִם מַכּוֹת."

═══ בי בה דו דום דום, בום בדום בום בו, בה דו, בה דה דום דום, דום דדום דום דום דום דום דום. בדה דו דום דדום. ═══

the suit, Jerry says,"that's a terrible deal...i'd rather make my own suit." Banya keeps trying to get more out of Jerry, and we are left to wonder if Banya would have been less needy had Jerry would have been more thankful at the onset. In both situations, Jerry learns the same thing the Haggadah is trying to teach us. We need to be overly and genuinely grateful for what was done for us, and through that gratitude we can deserve to continue to get positive developments.

The Invisible Being

When counting the amount of plagues, the Haggadah quotes the verse: "And Israel saw the Lord's great hand that He used upon the Egyptians, and the people feared the Lord; and they believed in the Lord, and in Moshe, His servant" (Exodus 14:31). The phrasing is odd. The Israelites see His hand, which makes them fear and believe in God Himself. How and why does this happen?

I believe something similar (albeit much more mundane) happens to us, the audience, with our good friend, Bob Sacamano.

THE HAGGADAH ABOUT NOTHING

Rabbi Akiva says, "From where can you derive that every plague that the Holy One, blessed be He, brought upon the Egyptians in Egypt was composed of five plagues? As it is stated (Psalms 78:49): 'He sent upon them the fierceness of His anger, wrath, and fury, and trouble, a sending of messengers of evil.' 'The fierceness of His anger' corresponds to one; 'wrath' brings it to two; 'and fury' brings it to three; 'and trouble' brings it to four; 'a sending of messengers of evil' brings it to five. You can say from here that in Egypt, they were struck with fifty plagues and at the Sea, they were struck with two hundred and fifty plagues."

===== BEE BA DO DUM DUM, BUM BADUM BUM BUH, BAH DUH, BAH DAH DUM DUM, DUM DEDUM DUM DUM DUM DUM. BADA DO DUM DEDUM. =====

In nine seasons we never meet Bob. He is mentioned in 10 episodes throughout the series, but we don't know what he looks or sounds like. However, we do see the invitations he sent to Jerry and late to Elaine[C120]. We see the fake sable hat Elaine tried to use to replace a real one[C121]. We see the bag of (defective) condoms he gives to Kramer[C122]. We also don't only have to take Kramer's name for it. In "The Chicken Roaster[C123]," when Jerry is living in Kramer's apartment he and Bob get to talking. We never meet Bob, we only see his hand.

Even with all the miracles going on, the Israelites still never see God. The times when they do are later. The Midrash notes that they saw the Divine Presence when going through the Red Sea and the Biblical account of Mt. Sinai. They, and religious people to this day, believe in God the same way we believe Bob Sacamano exists, by seeing the hand and acknowledging that the hand has an owner.

The Missing Leader

Moshe, who in many respects is the main character of the Exodus story in the Torah, is completely absent from the Haggadah other than this one time. When we told the story earlier he was absolutely nowhere to be found, and the Haggadah focuses on the nation, continually skipping his character's story. Moshe makes his only cameo here.

THE (UNOFFICIAL) SEINFELD HAGGADAH

רַבִּי עֲקִיבָא אוֹמֵר: "מִנַּיִן שֶׁכָּל־מַכָּה וּמַכָּה שֶׁהֵבִיא הַקָּדוֹשׁ בָּרוּךְ הוּא עַל הַמִּצְרִים בְּמִצְרַיִם הָיְתָה שֶׁל חָמֵשׁ מַכּוֹת? שֶׁנֶּאֱמַר (תהלים עח, מט): 'יְשַׁלַּח־בָּם חֲרוֹן אַפּוֹ, עֶבְרָה וָזַעַם וְצָרָה, מִשְׁלַחַת מַלְאֲכֵי רָעִים.' 'חֲרוֹן אַפּוֹ' – אַחַת, 'עֶבְרָה' – שְׁתַּיִם, 'וָזַעַם' – שָׁלוֹשׁ, 'וְצָרָה' – אַרְבַּע, 'מִשְׁלַחַת מַלְאֲכֵי רָעִים' – חָמֵשׁ. אֱמוֹר מֵעַתָּה: בְּמִצְרַיִם לָקוּ חֲמִשִּׁים מַכּוֹת וְעַל הַיָּם לָקוּ חֲמִשִּׁים וּמָאתַיִם מַכּוֹת."

בִּי בַּה דוּ דוּם דוּם, בּוּם בַּדוּם בּוּם בּוֹ, בַּה דוּ, בַּה דַּה דוּם דוּם, דוּם דַּדוּם דוּם דוּם דוּם דוּם. בַּדָה דוּ דוּם דַּדוּם.

It is similarly interesting that Larry David is largely absent in *Seinfeld*. He has 15 cameos throughout the series, but always as quick things, never as a true character in an episode. Given that Larry and Jerry wrote the show together, and Jerry is the main character, why is Larry so absent? It seems clear, based on how *Curb Your Enthusiasm* developed, that Larry is a huge character with a large personality. *Seinfeld* is balanced between the characters and Larry would loom too large shifting all the focus. We see this in *Curb*'s *Seinfeld* reunion episodes. When Larry tries to play George (George's character is largely based on Larry), it doesn't work because the focus is all on him.

Moshe similarly looms too large over the Exodus story. The story we want to tell on Seder night is one of a people, a nation, and how we fit into that history. Having Moshe present would shift the focus too much from us as a Jewish people. Therefore, he joins us, but only as a cameo.

DAYEINU

How many degrees of favors did the exalted One bestow upon us!

If He had taken us out of Egypt and not put the kibosh[65] upon them;   it would have been sufficient.
If He had put the kibosh on the Egyptians and not on their gods;   it would have been sufficient.
If He had executed judgments on their gods like a pitbull on a poodle[66] and had not slain their firstborn;
    it would have been sufficient.
If He had slain their firstborn and had not given us their wealth;   it would have been sufficient.

BEE BA DO DUM DUM, BUM BADUM BUM BUH, BAH DUH, BAH DAH DUM DUM, DUM DEDUM DUM DUM DUM DUM. BADA DO DUM DEDUM.

Kramer's Fantasy Dayeinu

Throughout the show, Kramer has a lot of jobs. They never seem to work out long term, so he always just moves onto the next one. At the same time he does seem to be able to support himself without any explanation. We say Dayenu to show we feel as lucky as Kramer should. As George notes in "The Visa[C124]:"

> "His [Kramer's] whole life is a fantasy camp. People should plunk down two thousand dollars to live like him for a week. Do nothing, fall a**-backwards into money, mooch food off your neighbors, and have sex without dating; that's a fantasy camp."

Therefore, it is only appropriate to list Dayeinu of many of the jobs Kramer had in the show.

If he had only been a inventor and not the CEO of Kramerica industries[C125], that would have been enough
If he had only been a CEO of Kramerica industries, and not a Woody Allen movie actor[C126], that would have been enough
If he had only been a Woody Allen movie actor, and not a sitcom

THE (UNOFFICIAL) SEINFELD HAGGADAH

דיינו

כַּמָה מַעֲלוֹת טוֹבוֹת לַמָקוֹם עָלֵינוּ!

אִלּוּ הוֹצִיאָנוּ מִמִצְרַיִם
וְלֹא עָשָׂה בָהֶם שְׁפָטִים, דַּיֵנוּ.
אִלּוּ עָשָׂה בָהֶם שְׁפָטִים,
וְלֹא עָשָׂה בֵאלֹהֵיהֶם, דַּיֵנוּ.
אִלּוּ עָשָׂה בֵאלֹהֵיהֶם,
וְלֹא הָרַג אֶת־בְּכוֹרֵיהֶם, דַּיֵנוּ.
אִלּוּ הָרַג אֶת־בְּכוֹרֵיהֶם,
וְלֹא נָתַן לָנוּ אֶת־מָמוֹנָם, דַּיֵנוּ.
אִלּוּ נָתַן לָנוּ אֶת־מָמוֹנָם,
וְלֹא קָרַע לָנוּ אֶת־הַיָם, דַּיֵנוּ.

> "I guarantee you that Moses was a picker. You wander through the desert for forty years with that dry air. You telling me you're not going to have occasion to clean house a little bit?"

בי בה דו דום דום, בום בדום בום בו, בה דו, בה דה דום דום, דום דדום דום דום דום דום. בדה דו דום דדום.

actor[C127], that would have been enough

If he had only been a sitcom actor, and not a model[C128] (underwear, portrait, smoking), that would have been enough

If he had only been a model, and not a screenwriter[C129], that would have been enough

If he had only been a screenwriter, and not a author[C130], that would have been enough

If he had only been a author, and not a reasturaunter[C131], that would have been enough

If he had only been a reasturaunter, and not a moviefone impersonator[C132], that would have been enough

מגיד — 89

THE HAGGADAH ABOUT NOTHING

If He had given us their wealth and had not split the sea for us;   it would have been sufficient.

If He had split the sea for us and had not taken us through it on dry land;   it would have been sufficient.

If He had taken us through it on dry land and had not pushed down our enemies into the sea; it would have been sufficient.

If He had pushed down our enemies into the sea and had not supplied our needs in the wilderness for forty years so we could tell Jewish jokes[67];   it would have been sufficient.

If He had supplied our needs in the wilderness for forty years and had not fed us the manna (instead of mutton[68]);
   it would have been sufficient.

If He had fed us the manna and had not given us the Shabbat;
   it would have been sufficient.

If He had given us the Shabbat and had not brought us close to Mount Sinai;   it would have been sufficient.

If He had brought us close to Mount Sinai and had not given us the Torah;   it would have been sufficient.

If He had given us the Torah and had not brought us into the land of Israel;   it would have been sufficient.

If He had brought us into the land of Israel and had not built us the Temple;   it would have been sufficient.

═ BEE BA DO DUM DUM, BUM BADUM BUM BUH, BAH DUH, BAH DAH DUM DUM, DUM DEDUM DUM DUM DUM DUM. BADA DO DUM DEDUM. ═

If he had only been a moviefone impersonator, and not a pretend medical patient[C133], that would have been enough

If he had only been a pretend medical patient, and not a photographer[C134], that would have been enough

If he had only been a photographer, and not a cigar/crepe manufacturer[C135], that would have been enough

If he had only been a cigar/crepe manufacturer, and not a rickshaw driver[C136], that would have been enough

If he had only been a rickshaw driver and not a bagel employee[C137],

90 — MAGGID

THE (UNOFFICIAL) SEINFELD HAGGADAH

	אִלּוּ קָרַע לָנוּ אֶת־הַיָּם,
דַּיֵּנוּ.	וְלֹא הֶעֱבִירָנוּ בְּתוֹכוֹ בֶּחָרָבָה,
	אִלּוּ הֶעֱבִירָנוּ בְּתוֹכוֹ בֶּחָרָבָה,
דַּיֵּנוּ.	וְלֹא שִׁקַּע צָרֵנוּ בְּתוֹכוֹ,
	אִלּוּ שִׁקַּע צָרֵנוּ בְּתוֹכוֹ,
דַּיֵּנוּ.	וְלֹא סִפֵּק צָרְכֵּנוּ בַּמִּדְבָּר אַרְבָּעִים שָׁנָה,
	אִלּוּ סִפֵּק צָרְכֵּנוּ בְּמִדְבָּר אַרְבָּעִים שָׁנָה,
דַּיֵּנוּ.	וְלֹא הֶאֱכִילָנוּ אֶת־הַמָּן,
	אִלּוּ הֶאֱכִילָנוּ אֶת־הַמָּן,
דַּיֵּנוּ.	וְלֹא נָתַן לָנוּ אֶת־הַשַּׁבָּת,
	אִלּוּ נָתַן לָנוּ אֶת־הַשַּׁבָּת,
דַּיֵּנוּ.	וְלֹא קֵרְבָנוּ לִפְנֵי הַר סִינַי,
	אִלּוּ קֵרְבָנוּ לִפְנֵי הַר סִינַי,
דַּיֵּנוּ.	וְלֹא נָתַן לָנוּ אֶת־הַתּוֹרָה.
	אִלּוּ נָתַן לָנוּ אֶת־הַתּוֹרָה,
דַּיֵּנוּ.	וְלֹא הִכְנִיסָנוּ לְאֶרֶץ יִשְׂרָאֵל,
	אִלּוּ הִכְנִיסָנוּ לְאֶרֶץ יִשְׂרָאֵל,
דַּיֵּנוּ.	וְלֹא בָנָה לָנוּ אֶת־בֵּית הַבְּחִירָה,

===== בִּי בַּה דוּ דוֹם דוּם, בּוֹם בְּדוֹם בּוֹם בּוֹ, בָּה דוּ, בַּה דָה דוּם דוּם, דוּם דְדוּם דוּם דוּם דוּם דוּם. בָּדָה דוּ דוּם דְדוּם. =====

that would have been enough

If he had only been a bagel maker, and not a party planner[C138], that would have been enough

If he had only been a party planner, and not a lifeguard[C139], that would have been enough

If he had only been a lifeguard, and not a tour creator[C140], that would have been enough

If he had only been a tour creator, and not a not actually office worker[C141], that would have been enough

מגיד — 91

How much greater then, incalculably great, are the benefits which the exalted God did confer upon us in double and redoubled measure! For he took us out of Egypt, and put the kibosh on them, and with their gods, and slain their firstborn, and gave us their wealth, and split the sea for us, and brought us through it on dry land, and pushed down our enemies into the sea, and supplied our needs in the wilderness for forty years, and fed us the manna, and gave us the Shabbat, and brought us close to Mount Sinai, and gave us the Torah, and brought us into the land of Israel and built us the Temple to atone upon all of our sins. All of these were million to one shot Doc, million to one[69].

RABBAN GAMLIEL'S THREE THINGS

Rabban Gamliel used to say, anyone who has not said these three things on Passover has not fulfilled his obligation, and these are them: the Passover sacrifice, matzah and maror.

BEE BA DO DUM DUM, BUM BADUM BUM BUH, BAH DUH, BAH DAH DUM DUM, DUM DEDUM DUM DUM DUM DUM. BADA DO DUM DEDUM.

The Friend's Pesach

Everything about the ancient Paschal Sacrifice during the Exodus in the Torah revolves around the home. The home's focus is evidenced by the laws prescribed in the text: each house's doorposts were painted with blood, the sacrifice was required to be eaten in the home, and the meat itself becomes unfit if it leaves the house. Pesach as a holiday continues this tradition, primarily by being a holiday celebrated around a table in a home and with family. To relay the national heritage, it must happen specifically, family by family.

On some level, Jerry's apartment functions like the ancient home in *Seinfeld*. The characters are always going back to it, a perpetual if not eternal meeting place. Sometimes, the characters just show up, assuming Jerry will be home, which he usually is. They rarely

THE (UNOFFICIAL) SEINFELD HAGGADAH

עַל אַחַת, כַּמָּה וְכַמָּה, טוֹבָה כְפוּלָה וּמְכֻפֶּלֶת לַמָּקוֹם עָלֵינוּ! שֶׁהוֹצִיאָנוּ מִמִּצְרַיִם, וְעָשָׂה בָהֶם שְׁפָטִים, וְעָשָׂה בֵאלֹהֵיהֶם, וְהָרַג אֶת־בְּכוֹרֵיהֶם, וְנָתַן לָנוּ אֶת־מָמוֹנָם, וְקָרַע לָנוּ אֶת־הַיָּם, וְהֶעֱבִירָנוּ בְתוֹכוֹ בֶּחָרָבָה, וְשִׁקַּע צָרֵנוּ בְּתוֹכוֹ, וְסִפֵּק צָרְכֵּנוּ בַּמִּדְבָּר אַרְבָּעִים שָׁנָה, וְהֶאֱכִילָנוּ אֶת־הַמָּן, וְנָתַן לָנוּ אֶת־הַשַּׁבָּת, וְקֵרְבָנוּ לִפְנֵי הַר סִינַי, וְנָתַן לָנוּ אֶת־הַתּוֹרָה, וְהִכְנִיסָנוּ לְאֶרֶץ יִשְׂרָאֵל, וּבָנָה לָנוּ אֶת־בֵּית הַבְּחִירָה לְכַפֵּר עַל־כָּל־עֲוֹנוֹתֵינוּ.

רבן גמליאל היה אומר

רַבָּן גַּמְלִיאֵל הָיָה אוֹמֵר: כָּל שֶׁלֹּא אָמַר שְׁלֹשָׁה דְבָרִים אֵלּוּ בַּפֶּסַח, לֹא יָצָא יְדֵי חוֹבָתוֹ, וְאֵלּוּ הֵן: פֶּסַח, מַצָּה, וּמָרוֹר.

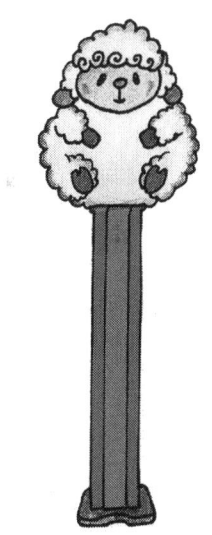

פֶּסַח שֶׁהָיוּ אֲבוֹתֵינוּ אוֹכְלִים בִּזְמַן שֶׁבֵּית הַמִּקְדָּשׁ הָיָה קַיָּם, עַל שׁוּם מָה? עַל שׁוּם שֶׁפָּסַח הַקָּדוֹשׁ בָּרוּךְ הוּא עַל

בי בה דו דום דום, בום בדום בום בו, בה דו, בה דה דום דום, דום דדום דום דום דום דום. בדה דו דום דדום.

have their meals there, but they always eat in Monk's nearby, which functions essentially as Jerry's dining room. The main difference between the Pesach home and Jerry's apartment is who fills them. Pesach happens primarily with family, Jerry has his friends. This is not accidental, his friends are the locus of his life. He even describes how wonderful it is to have a 1200 mile "buffer zone" from his family in

THE HAGGADAH ABOUT NOTHING

What is the reason for the Passover sacrifice that our ancestors ate when the Temple existed? It is to commemorate that the Holy One, blessed be He, passed over the homes of our ancestors in Egypt, as it is stated (Exodus 12:27), "And you shall say: 'It is the Passover sacrifice to the Lord, for that He passed over the homes of the Children of Israel in Egypt, when He smote the Egyptians, and our homes He saved.' And the people bowed their heads and bowed."

Hold the matzah and display it.

What is the reason for the matzah that we eat? To commemorate that our ancestors' dough was not yet able to rise, before the King of kings, the Holy One, blessed be He, revealed Himself to them and redeemed them, as it is stated (Exodus 12:39), "And they baked the dough which they brought out of Egypt into matzah cakes, since it did not rise; because they were expelled from Egypt, and could not tarry, neither had they made for themselves provisions." So they ran (like a man, with their knees up[70]) like they were pretending there's like, murderers chasing you, and you try and see how fast you can get your keys out and get into your apartment[71].

═ BEE BA DO DUM DUM, BUM BADUM BUM BUH, BAH DUH, BAH DAH DUM DUM, DUM DEDUM DUM DUM DUM DUM. BADA DO DUM DEDUM. ═

Florida[C142]. This is not to say Jerry doesn't love his family in the show, he certainly does, but the focus of his life is his friends, not his family. The same is evermore true with Geroge, Elaine, and Kramer who have more complicated relationships with their families. At the same time, these characters have created a family, not by blood, but from shared experience. On Pesach, we try to add to our family structure what our characters have in Jerry's apartment. We try to extend past our blood families to the entire nation of Israel. We therefore must discuss the Pesach because Pesach is a commandment of our homes and our homes are intrinsically linked to our national experience.

94 — MAGGID

בָּתֵּי אֲבוֹתֵינוּ בְּמִצְרַיִם, שֶׁנֶּאֱמַר: "וַאֲמַרְתֶּם (שמות יב, כז): 'זֶבַח פֶּסַח הוּא לַה', אֲשֶׁר פָּסַח עַל בָּתֵּי בְנֵי יִשְׂרָאֵל בְּמִצְרַיִם בְּנָגְפּוֹ אֶת־מִצְרַיִם, וְאֶת־בָּתֵּינוּ הִצִּיל.' וַיִּקֹּד הָעָם וַיִּשְׁתַּחֲווּ."

Hold the matzah and display it.

מַצָּה זוֹ שֶׁאָנוּ אוֹכְלִים, עַל שׁוּם מַה? עַל שׁוּם שֶׁלֹּא הִסְפִּיק בְּצֵקָם שֶׁל אֲבוֹתֵינוּ לְהַחֲמִיץ עַד שֶׁנִּגְלָה עֲלֵיהֶם מֶלֶךְ מַלְכֵי הַמְּלָכִים, הַקָּדוֹשׁ בָּרוּךְ הוּא, וּגְאָלָם, שֶׁנֶּאֱמַר (שמות יב, לט): "וַיֹּאפוּ אֶת־הַבָּצֵק אֲשֶׁר הוֹצִיאוּ מִמִּצְרַיִם עֻגֹת מַצּוֹת, כִּי לֹא חָמֵץ, כִּי גֹרְשׁוּ מִמִּצְרַיִם וְלֹא יָכְלוּ לְהִתְמַהְמֵהַּ, וְגַם צֵדָה לֹא עָשׂוּ לָהֶם."

THREE SQUARES?
YOU CAN'T SPARE THREE SQUARES?

בי בה דו דום דום, בום בדום בום בו, בה דו, בה דה דום דום, דום דדום דום דום דום דום דום. בדה דו דום דדום.

The Worried Matzah

The Torah gives us a different name for the holiday than the one we are accustomed to. We usually call it Pesach/Passover, but the Torah primarily calls it the Festival of Matzahs. The Chassidic Rebbe, Rabbi Levi of Berditchev, notes that this is dependent on perspective. For us, it's Pesach because we are thankful to God for passing over our houses. God on the other hand, is noting that we were willing to leave Egypt with our bread before it was ready. We were willing to follow Him without worrying about where our food is coming from. The Torah sees this as so significant it names the holiday after it.

Hold the maror and display it.

What is the reason for this maror that we are eating? To commemorate that the Egyptians embittered the lives of our ancestors in Egypt, as it is stated (Exodus 1:14); "And they made their lives bitter with hard service, in mortar and in brick, and in all manner of service in the field; in all their service, wherein they made them serve with rigor."

<small>BA DO DUM DUM, BUM BADUM BUM BUH, BAH DUH, BAH DAH DUM DUM, DUM DEDUM DUM DUM DUM DUM. BADA DO DUM DEDUM.</small>

As discussed so many times in this particular Haggadah, the characters are always worrying. They are neurotic to the point of exhaustion. So much so, that there have been plenty of articles written regarding watchers of *Seinfeld* taking on some of the neuroses. The Torah is praising fleeing people for forgoing worrying in a time when it was perfectly reasonable, if not downright prudent, to worry. Therefore, matzah becomes integral to the Exodus, and one of the three things we must discuss. It was our main part in leaving Egypt, and this is our story after all. We can only hope Jerry would have stopped worrying while leaving. At least he is "the Master Packer"[C143]."

The Small Bitters

George has a hard time throughout *Seinfeld*. It is usually assumed that he is the loser of the group, or, as Jerry calls him, the "Biff"[C144] from *Death of a Salesman*. In "The Andrea Doria"[C145]," George's despair is brought to the foreground. George wants to get a new apartment, but the board of the building is planning on giving it to a survivor of the Andrea Doria shipwreck. When complaining to Jerry, Jerry makes George realize that he's had much more pain than that overall and should use the pain for good:

> GEORGE: So, he's keeping the apartment. He doesn't deserve it, though! Even if he did suffer, that was, like, 40 years ago! What has he been doing lately?! I've been suffering for the past 30 years up to and including yesterday!
> JERRY: You know, if this tenant board is so impressed with suffering, maybe you should tell them the "Astonishing Tales of Costanza."
> GEORGE: (Interested) I should!
> JERRY: I mean, your body of work in this field is unparalleled.
> GEORGE: I could go bumper to bumper with anyone else on this planet!
> JERRY: You're the man!

THE (UNOFFICIAL) SEINFELD HAGGADAH

Hold the maror and display it.

מָרוֹר זֶה שֶׁאָנוּ אוֹכְלִים, עַל שׁוּם מַה? עַל שׁוּם שֶׁמֵּרְרוּ הַמִּצְרִים אֶת־חַיֵּי אֲבוֹתֵינוּ בְּמִצְרַיִם, שֶׁנֶּאֱמַר (שמות א, יד): "וַיְמָרֲרוּ אֶת חַיֵּיהֶם בַּעֲבֹדָה קָשָׁה, בְּחֹמֶר וּבִלְבֵנִים וּבְכָל־עֲבֹדָה בַּשָּׂדֶה אֵת כָּל עֲבֹדָתָם אֲשֶׁר עָבְדוּ בָהֶם בְּפָרֶךְ."

בִּי בה דו דום דום, בום בדום בום בו, בה דו, בה דה דום דום, דום דדום דום דום דום. בדה דו דום דדום.

George makes the board cry with his extensive list of excruciating minor encounters, ending it off with the devastating fact that his fiancee died by licking the envelopes to their wedding that he picked out. If only one time, George realizes that he can use his pain for good.

Rabbi Norman Lamm, an influential American Modern Orthodox scholar, notes that we recite a blessing over the maror because we acknowledge that even from the most bitter things we can extract blessings. As he writes: "Indeed, the beauty of the Seder in its teaching of the bitter sweet quality of life and the meaningfulness of suffering, but the further fact that evil itself is the source from which the good can be fashioned." Like George in this episode, we used our slavery to learn how to become a people together and for God. The maror is integral to the Seder because we must learn to not only celebrate being saved in Egypt with the Pesach, and getting taken out with the matzah, but also the initial pain that enabled the redemption with the maror. George is only able to appreciate his pain when realizing it will benefit him practically, but we bless the maror to remember it can (sometimes) benefit us spiritually also.

מגיד — 97

In each and every generation, a person is obligated to see themselves as if they left Egypt, as it is stated (Exodus 13:8), "And you shall explain to your son on that day: For the sake of this, did the Lord do this for me in my going out of Egypt." Not only our ancestors did the Holy One, blessed be He, redeem, but rather together with them did He redeem us, as it is stated (Deuteronomy 6:23), "And He took us out from there, in order to bring us in, to give us the land which He swore unto our fathers."

FIRST HALF OF HALLEL

Cover the matzot and raise the cup of wine.

Therefore we are obligated to thank, praise, laud, glorify, exalt, lavish, bless, raise high, and acclaim He who made all these miracles for our ancestors and for us: He brought us out from slavery to freedom, from sorrow to joy, from mourning to celebration of a festival, from darkness to great light, and from servitude to redemption. And let us say a new song before Him, Halleluyah!

BEE BA DO DUM DUM, BUM BADUM BUM BUH, BAH DUH, BAH DAH DUM DUM, DUM DEDUM DUM DUM DUM DUM. BADA DO DUM DEDUM.

The Maggid Finale

It wasn't a foregone conclusion that *Seinfeld* would be a hit. The show opened to lukewarm reviews, and an NBC internal report dubbed the pilot as "weak." Larry David himself reminisced how after the pilot he told Jerry that he was "thinking that [he] wouldn't see [him] again for another couple of years." Nine years later, *Seinfeld* couldn't have been more popular. 76 million people tuned into the finale, and is still so popular that someone who was a kid when the show was on, and didn't watch it until college, is making a Haggadah about it (and you're reading it!). *Seinfeld*, like the Seder, begins with shame and ends with praise.

THE (UNOFFICIAL) SEINFELD HAGGADAH

בְּכָל־דּוֹר וָדוֹר חַיָּב אָדָם לִרְאוֹת אֶת־עַצְמוֹ כְּאִלּוּ הוּא יָצָא מִמִּצְרַיִם, שֶׁנֶּאֱמַר (שמות יג, ח): וְהִגַּדְתָּ לְבִנְךָ בַּיּוֹם הַהוּא לֵאמֹר, בַּעֲבוּר זֶה עָשָׂה ה' לִי בְּצֵאתִי מִמִּצְרָיִם. לֹא אֶת־אֲבוֹתֵינוּ בִּלְבָד גָּאַל הַקָּדוֹשׁ בָּרוּךְ הוּא, אֶלָּא אַף אוֹתָנוּ גָּאַל עִמָּהֶם, שֶׁנֶּאֱמַר (דברים ו, כג): וְאוֹתָנוּ הוֹצִיא מִשָּׁם, לְמַעַן הָבִיא אוֹתָנוּ, לָתֶת לָנוּ אֶת־הָאָרֶץ אֲשֶׁר נִשְׁבַּע לַאֲבֹתֵינוּ.

חצי הלל

Cover the matzot and raise the cup of wine.

לְפִיכָךְ אֲנַחְנוּ חַיָּבִים לְהוֹדוֹת, לְהַלֵּל, לְשַׁבֵּחַ, לְפָאֵר, לְרוֹמֵם, לְהַדֵּר, לְבָרֵךְ, לְעַלֵּה וּלְקַלֵּס לְמִי שֶׁעָשָׂה לַאֲבוֹתֵינוּ וְלָנוּ אֶת־כָּל־הַנִסִּים הָאֵלּוּ: הוֹצִיאָנוּ מֵעַבְדוּת לְחֵרוּת. מִיָּגוֹן לְשִׂמְחָה, וּמֵאֵבֶל לְיוֹם טוֹב, וּמֵאֲפֵלָה לְאוֹר גָּדוֹל, וּמִשִּׁעְבּוּד לִגְאֻלָּה. וְנֹאמַר לְפָנָיו שִׁירָה חֲדָשָׁה, הַלְלוּיָהּ!

מגיד — 99

THE HAGGADAH ABOUT NOTHING

Halleluyah! Give praise, O servants of the Lord, praise the name of the Lord. May the Name of the Lord be blessed from now and forever. From the rising of the sun in the East to its setting, the name of the Lord is praised. Above all nations is the Lord, His honor is above the heavens. Who is like the Lord, our God, Who sits on high; Who looks down upon the heavens and the earth? He brings up the poor out of the dirt; from the refuse piles, He raises the destitute. To seat him with the nobles, with the nobles of his people. He seats a barren woman in a home, a happy mother of children. Halleluyah! (Psalms 113)

═ BEE BA DO DUM DUM, BUM BADUM BUM BUH, BAH DUH, BAH DAH DUM DUM, DUM DEDUM DUM DUM DUM DUM. BADA DO DUM DEDUM. ═

Maharal, the 16th century Czech philosopher, in his "Netzach Yisrael," teaches us that "a proper awareness of the greatness of a matter becomes known through its opposite." We start with shame so that praise is clear. Had we just talked about the Exodus without starting with the slavery, it would be harder to appreciate the freedom at story's close, a freedom we still celebrate from within. Similarly, if we talked about becoming God's people without discussing our crumbling sense of peoplehood in Egypt, the magnitude would be missed. *Seinfeld*, for all its continued popularity, was not treated with hype when it began. Thankfully, the writers and actors persevered and continued writing. Now that seems obvious, but at the time it likely did not, and for that, we should see their achievements as even greater than those of other comedies.

The Eating Hallel

We begin Hallel before the meal and finish it afterwards. In all other situations, Hallel is said as one unit, not in two separate parts. Aside from not wanting to wait for the meal like we're waiting for a table at a Chinese restaurant, why do we not say Hallel in concurrently? Many commentaries point out that Hallel is split into two purposely. Before the meal, the Haggadah focuses on the redemption in the past in Egypt. Afterward the meal, we hope for the future redemption. The beginning of Hallel, which deals mostly

THE (UNOFFICIAL) SEINFELD HAGGADAH

הַלְלוּיָהּ הַלְלוּ עַבְדֵי ה', הַלְלוּ אֶת־שֵׁם ה'. יְהִי שֵׁם ה' מְבֹרָךְ מֵעַתָּה וְעַד עוֹלָם. מִמִּזְרַח שֶׁמֶשׁ עַד מְבוֹאוֹ מְהֻלָּל שֵׁם ה'. רָם עַל־כָּל־גּוֹיִם ה', עַל הַשָּׁמַיִם כְּבוֹדוֹ. מִי כַּה' אֱלֹהֵינוּ הַמַּגְבִּיהִי לָשָׁבֶת, הַמַּשְׁפִּילִי לִרְאוֹת בַּשָּׁמַיִם וּבָאָרֶץ? מְקִימִי מֵעָפָר דָּל, מֵאַשְׁפֹּת יָרִים אֶבְיוֹן, לְהוֹשִׁיבִי עִם־נְדִיבִים, עִם נְדִיבֵי עַמּוֹ. מוֹשִׁיבִי עֲקֶרֶת הַבַּיִת, אֵם הַבָּנִים שְׂמֵחָה. הַלְלוּיָהּ. (תהלים קיג)

בי בה דו דום דום, בום בדום בום בו, בה דו, בה דה דום דום, דום דדום דום דום דום דום. בדה דו דום דדום.

with the Exodus precedes the meal. The end of Hallel, which relates to future redemptions, goes afterwards. But why separate it with the food and the meal? An answer can be found in Jerry's response to George when George isn't sure how he feels about a girl.

In "The Mango[C146]," Jerry asks: "All right, let me ask you this: when she comes over, you're cleaning up a lot?" and specifically "You do the tub?" When George affirms that he cleans up when she comes over, Jerry's response is: "tub is love." Jerry can truly see what the relationship means not through what George says or feels, but through what he actually does. The menial actions he takes to impress her is a far better indicator than anything else.

The Seder's focus is on the Exodus and the surrounding rituals, but eating a festive meal can be equally important. It is one thing to praise God through our voices, but another to act out thankfulness by having a special meal. The meal, therefore, is integral to the Seder because it is our tub, so to speak, and tub is love.

When Israel came out from Egypt, the house of Yaakov from a people of foreign speech. Yehudah became His sanctuary, Israel, His dominion. The sea saw it, and fled because it was angry that day my friends[72], the Jordan turned to the rear. The mountains danced like rams, like a full body dry heave set to music[73], the hills like young sheep. What ails you, O sea, that you are fleeing, Jordan that you turn to the rear? You mountains that you dance like rams, and you hills like young sheep? From before the Master, tremble you, earth, from before the Lord of Yaakov. He who turns the boulder into a pond of water, the flint into a spring of water. (Psalms 114)

SECOND CUP OF WINE

We raise the cup for the second cup of wine.

Blessed are You, Lord our God, King of the universe, who redeemed us and redeemed our ancestors from Egypt, and brought us on this night to eat matzah and maror; so too, Lord our God, and God of our ancestors, bring us to other appointed times and holidays that will come to greet us in peace, joyful in the building of Your city and happy in Your worship; that we shall eat there from the offerings and from the Passover sacrifices, the blood of which shall reach the wall of Your altar for favor, and we shall thank You with a new song upon our redemption and upon the restoration of our souls. Blessed are you, Lord, who redeemed Israel.

Blessed are You, Lord our God, King of the Universe, who creates the fruit of the vine.

THE (UNOFFICIAL) SEINFELD HAGGADAH

בְּצֵאת יִשְׂרָאֵל מִמִּצְרָיִם, בֵּית יַעֲקֹב מֵעַם לֹעֵז, הָיְתָה יְהוּדָה לְקָדְשׁוֹ, יִשְׂרָאֵל מַמְשְׁלוֹתָיו. הַיָּם רָאָה וַיָּנֹס, הַיַּרְדֵּן יִסֹּב לְאָחוֹר. הֶהָרִים רָקְדוּ כְאֵילִים, גְּבָעוֹת כִּבְנֵי צֹאן. מַה לְּךָ הַיָּם כִּי תָנוּס, הַיַּרְדֵּן – תִּסֹּב לְאָחוֹר, הֶהָרִים – תִּרְקְדוּ כְאֵילִים, גְּבָעוֹת כִּבְנֵי־צֹאן. מִלִּפְנֵי אָדוֹן חוּלִי אָרֶץ, מִלִּפְנֵי אֱלוֹהַּ יַעֲקֹב. הַהֹפְכִי הַצּוּר אֲגַם־מָיִם, חַלָּמִישׁ לְמַעְיְנוֹ־מָיִם. (תהלים קיד)

כוס שניה

We raise the cup for the second cup of wine.

בָּרוּךְ אַתָּה ה' אֱלֹהֵינוּ מֶלֶךְ הָעוֹלָם, אֲשֶׁר גְּאָלָנוּ וְגָאַל אֶת־אֲבוֹתֵינוּ מִמִּצְרַיִם, וְהִגִּיעָנוּ הַלַּיְלָה הַזֶּה לֶאֱכָל־בּוֹ מַצָּה וּמָרוֹר. כֵּן ה' אֱלֹהֵינוּ וֵאלֹהֵי אֲבוֹתֵינוּ יַגִּיעֵנוּ לְמוֹעֲדִים וְלִרְגָלִים אֲחֵרִים הַבָּאִים לִקְרָאתֵנוּ לְשָׁלוֹם, שְׂמֵחִים בְּבִנְיַן עִירֶךָ וְשָׂשִׂים בַּעֲבוֹדָתֶךָ. וְנֹאכַל שָׁם מִן הַזְּבָחִים וּמִן הַפְּסָחִים אֲשֶׁר יַגִּיעַ דָּמָם עַל קִיר מִזְבַּחֲךָ לְרָצוֹן, וְנוֹדֶה לְךָ שִׁיר חָדָשׁ עַל גְּאֻלָּתֵנוּ וְעַל פְּדוּת נַפְשֵׁנוּ. בָּרוּךְ אַתָּה ה', גָּאַל יִשְׂרָאֵל.

בָּרוּךְ אַתָּה ה', אֱלֹהֵינוּ מֶלֶךְ הָעוֹלָם, בּוֹרֵא פְּרִי הַגָּפֶן.

Washing

We wash our hands and make the blessing.

Blessed are You, Lord our God, King of the Universe, who has sanctified us with His commandments and has commanded us on the washing of the hands.

Motzi Matzah

Raise the 3 matzot and recite the first blessing. Put back down the bottom matzah and then recite the second blessing. While saying the second blessing have the Korekh sandwich in mind. Matzah is eaten while leaning to the left.

Blessed are You, Lord our God, King of the Universe, who brings forth bread (including marble rye[74]) from the ground.

Blessed are You, Lord our God, King of the Universe, who has sanctified us with His commandments and has commanded us on the eating of matzah.

=== BEE BA DO DUM DUM, BUM BADUM BUM BUH, BAH DUH, BAH DAH DUM DUM, DUM DEDUM DUM DUM DUM DUM. BADA DO DUM DEDUM. ===

The Lent Tupperware of Matzah

There is an idea quoted that each person must own the matzah that they eat at the Seder. The Sfas Emes (Succah 35), the 19th century Polish Chassidic writer, quotes this idea, but notes that this practice is not being followed. Rav Asher Weiss, a modern Halakhic decisor, explains that this practice is not followed because it is not necessary. At the Seder, each person is handed a matzah to eat. Rav Asher Weiss clarifies that when you give someone something that can only be used in a way that it is consumed and can't be returned,

THE (UNOFFICIAL) SEINFELD HAGGADAH

רָחְצָה

We wash our hands and make the blessing.

בָּרוּךְ אַתָּה ה', אֱלֹהֵינוּ מֶלֶךְ הָעוֹלָם, אֲשֶׁר קִדְּשָׁנוּ בְּמִצְוֹתָיו וְצִוָּנוּ עַל נְטִילַת יָדַיִם.

מוֹצִיא מַצָּה

Raise the 3 matzot and recite the first blessing. Put back down the bottom matzah and then recite the second blessing. While saying the second blessing have the Korekh sandwich in mind. Matzah is eaten while leaning to the left.

בָּרוּךְ אַתָּה ה', אֱלֹהֵינוּ מֶלֶךְ הָעוֹלָם, הַמּוֹצִיא לֶחֶם מִן הָאָרֶץ.

בָּרוּךְ אַתָּה ה', אֱלֹהֵינוּ מֶלֶךְ הָעוֹלָם, אֲשֶׁר קִדְּשָׁנוּ בְּמִצְוֹתָיו וְצִוָּנוּ עַל אֲכִילַת מַצָּה.

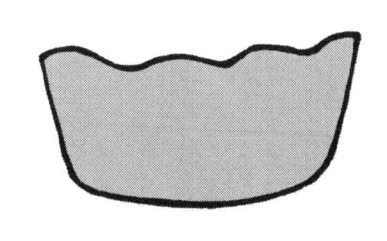

it is implied that it is now theirs. The transfer of ownership needs no explication. So, if you give someone food, or a single use item, it is implied that you gave over ownership. Therefore, when the host gives a guest a piece of matzah, it is implied the matzah is the guest's now. However, if the item is not consumed then any legal transfer must be made explicitly.

Kramer appears to hold like Rav Asher Weiss. In "The Kiss Hello[C147]," Kramer packs up leftover Chinese food and gives it to a homeless person, asking if he "will be there in an hour." Kramer returns and asks for his tupperware. When the homeless man refuses,

═══ BEE BA DO DUM DUM, BUM BADUM BUM BUH, BAH DUH, BAH DAH DUM DUM, DUM DEDUM DUM DUM DUM DUM. BADA DO DUM DEDUM. ═══

Maror

All present should take a kazayit of maror, dip into the haroset, make the blessing and eat without reclining because it is supposed to be bitter. Even though, if you think about it, maror can be quite good. Ma is good, roar is good, when you consider the other choices, maror is pretty refreshing[75].

Blessed are You, Lord our God, King of the Universe, who has sanctified us with His commandments and has commanded us on the eating of maror.

Wrap

All present should take a kazayit from the third whole matzah with a kazayit of maror, wrap them together into a sandwich and eat them while reclining and without saying a blessing. Before you eat, say:

In memory of the Temple according to Hillel. This is what Hillel would do when the Temple existed: He would wrap the matzah and maror and eat them together, in order to fulfill what is stated, (Exodus 12:15): "You should eat it upon matzot and bitter herbs."

THE (UNOFFICIAL) SEINFELD HAGGADAH

they have the following exchange:

> KRAMER: No, no, I didn't say you could keep it. You see I don't give away tupperware.
> HOMELESS MAN: You should have said something.
> KRAMER: I didn't think I had to. Look with a piece of Tupperware you just assume.

Clearly, Kramer meant to give the Chinese food inside the tupperware because the Chinese food is consumed. However, because the tupperware can be reused, it needed to be an explicit transfer of ownership. It appears Rav Asher Weiss would agree.

בי בה דו דום דום, בום בדום בום בן, בה די, בה דה דום דום, דום דדום דום דום דום, בדה דו דום דדום.

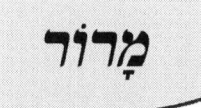

מָרוֹר

All present should take a kazayit of maror, dip into the haroset, make the blessing and eat without reclining because it is supposed to be bitter. Even though, if you think about it, maror can be quite good. Ma is good, roar is good, when you consider the other choices, maror is pretty refreshing.

בָּרוּךְ אַתָּה ה', אֱלֹהֵינוּ מֶלֶךְ הָעוֹלָם, אֲשֶׁר קִדְּשָׁנוּ בְּמִצְוֹתָיו וְצִוָּנוּ עַל אֲכִילַת מָרוֹר.

כּוֹרֵךְ

All present should take a kazayit from the third whole matzah with a kazayit of maror, wrap them together into a sandwich and eat them while reclining and without saying a blessing. Before you eat, say:

זֵכֶר לְמִקְדָּשׁ כְּהִלֵּל. כֵּן עָשָׂה הִלֵּל בִּזְמַן שֶׁבֵּית הַמִּקְדָּשׁ הָיָה קַיָּם. הָיָה כּוֹרֵךְ מַצָּה וּמָרוֹר וְאוֹכֵל בְּיַחַד, לְקַיֵּם מַה שֶׁנֶּאֱמַר: עַל מַצּוֹת וּמְרוֹרִים יֹאכְלֻהוּ.

Shulchan Orech

The Festive Meal is now eaten.

The Concealed [Matzah]

After the end of the meal, take the matzah that was hidden earlier. The afikoman must be eaten before Halakhic midnight.

```
ORIGINAL  SCHNITZER'S   CAFE
874-8755  MAZO BAKERY  874-8643
```

THE (UNOFFICIAL) SEINFELD HAGGADAH

שֻׁלְחָן עוֹרֵךְ

The Festive Meal is now eaten.

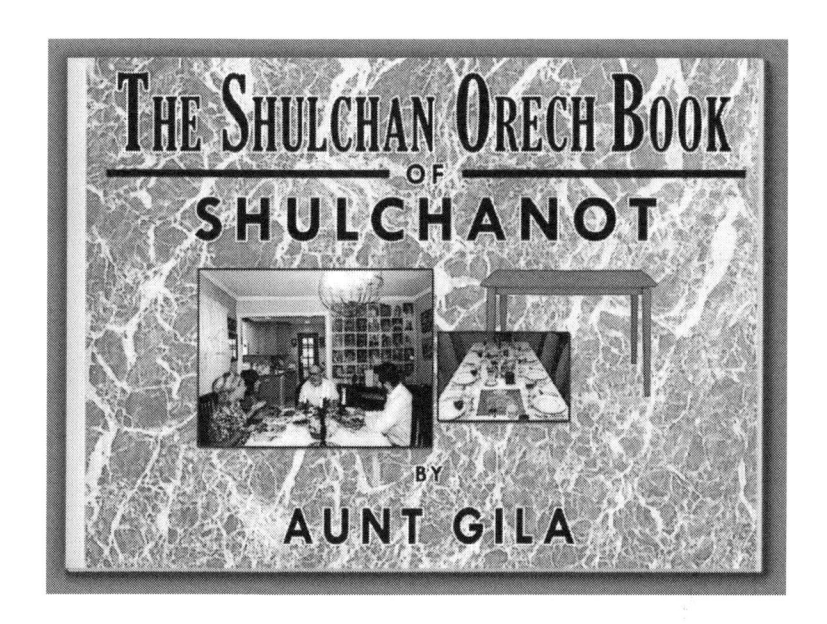

THE SHULCHAN ORECH BOOK OF SHULCHANOT

BY AUNT GILA

צָפוּן

After the end of the meal, take the matzah that was hidden earlier. The afikoman must be eaten before Halakhic midnight.

Bless

We pour the third cup and recite the Grace after Meals.

A Song of Ascents; When the Lord will return the captivity of Zion, we will be like dreamers that a hamburger was eating us![76] Then our mouth will be full of laughter and our tongue joyful melody. Then they will declare among the nations; "The Lord has done greatly with these." The Lord has done great things with us; we are happy. Lord, return our captivity like streams in the desert. Those that sow with tears will reap with joyful song. He who surely goes and cries, he carries the measure of seed, he will surely come in joyful song and carry his sheaves. (Psalms 126)

Three men or three women that ate together are obligated to introduce Grace after Meals. If 10 or more men are present the additions in brackets are added. The leader of the introduction opens as follows:

My masters/friends, let us bless.

All those present answer: May the Name of the Lord be blessed from now and forever. (Psalms 113:2)

The leader says: May the Name of the Lord be blessed from now and forever. With the permission of our gentlemen and our teachers and my masters, let us bless [our God] from whom we have eaten.

Those present answer: Blessed is [our God] from whom we have eaten and from whose goodness we live.

The leader says: Blessed is [our God] from whom we have eaten and from whose goodness we live.

בָּרֵךְ

We pour the third cup and recite the Grace after Meals.

שִׁיר הַמַּעֲלוֹת, בְּשׁוּב ה' אֶת שִׁיבַת צִיּוֹן הָיִינוּ כְּחֹלְמִים. אָז יִמָּלֵא שְׂחוֹק פִּינוּ וּלְשׁוֹנֵנוּ רִנָּה. אָז יֹאמְרוּ בַגּוֹיִם: הִגְדִּיל ה' לַעֲשׂוֹת עִם אֵלֶּה. הִגְדִּיל ה' לַעֲשׂוֹת עִמָּנוּ, הָיִינוּ שְׂמֵחִים. שׁוּבָה ה' אֶת שְׁבִיתֵנוּ כַּאֲפִיקִים בַּנֶּגֶב. הַזֹּרְעִים בְּדִמְעָה, בְּרִנָּה יִקְצֹרוּ. הָלוֹךְ יֵלֵךְ וּבָכֹה נֹשֵׂא מֶשֶׁךְ הַזָּרַע, בֹּא יָבֹא בְרִנָּה נֹשֵׂא אֲלֻמֹּתָיו. (תהלים קכו)

Three men or three women that ate together are obligated to introduce Grace after Meals. If 10 or more men are present the additions in brackets are added. The leader of the introduction opens as follows:

רַבּוֹתַי/חֲבֵרַי נְבָרֵךְ.

All those present answer:

יְהִי שֵׁם ה' מְבֹרָךְ מֵעַתָּה וְעַד עוֹלָם. (תהלים קיג, ב)

The leader says:

יְהִי שֵׁם ה' מְבֹרָךְ מֵעַתָּה וְעַד עוֹלָם. בִּרְשׁוּת מָרָנָן וְרַבָּנָן וְרַבּוֹתַי, נְבָרֵךְ [אֱלֹהֵינוּ] שֶׁאָכַלְנוּ מִשֶּׁלּוֹ.

Those present answer:

בָּרוּךְ [אֱלֹהֵינוּ] שֶׁאָכַלְנוּ מִשֶּׁלּוֹ וּבְטוּבוֹ חָיִינוּ.

The leader says:

בָּרוּךְ [אֱלֹהֵינוּ] שֶׁאָכַלְנוּ מִשֶּׁלּוֹ וּבְטוּבוֹ חָיִינוּ.

All say:

Blessed are You, Lord our God, King of the universe, who feeds the whole world with His goodness, with grace, with kindness and with mercy. He gives bread to all flesh, for His kindness is eternal, and in His great goodness we never lack, nor will we lack food forever for the sake of His great Name, because He is a God who feeds and sustains all and is beneficial to all, and prepares food for all of His creatures including Jewish delicacies for 183 Jewish singles[77] whom He created. Blessed are You, Lord, who feeds all.

We thank you, Lord our God, that you have given as an inheritance to our ancestors a lovely, good and broad land, and that You took us out, Lord our God, from the land of Egypt and that You redeemed us from a house of slaves,

══ BEE BA DO DUM DUM, BUM BADUM BUM BUH, BAH DUH, BAH DAH DUM DUM, DUM DEDUM DUM DUM DUM DUM. BADA DO DUM DEDUM. ══

The Graceful Grace

In "The Chaperone[C148]," Elaine is lectured on having "grace" while interviewing for an employer. Their discussion goes as follows:

> LANDIS (the interviewer): Not many people have grace.
> ELAINE: Well, you know, grace is a tough one. I like to think I have a little grace...not as much as Jackie—
> LANDIS: You can't have "a little grace." You either have grace, or you...don't.
> ELAINE: O.K., fine, I have... no grace.
> LANDIS: And you can't acquire grace.
> ELAINE: Well, I have no intention of "getting" grace.
> LANDIS: Grace isn't something you can pick up at the market.
> ELAINE (fed up): Alright, alright, look — I don't have grace, I don't want grace... I don't even say grace, O.K.?

Landis argues that grace is something that one has or doesn't have. Grace is an inborn and innate quality, one that fully exists in the person or not. Later in the episode, Mr. Pitt, who becomes Elaine's employer, says she exhibits "some grace," gratifying Elaine.

Jewish tradition largely disagrees with Landis. Grace is

THE (UNOFFICIAL) SEINFELD HAGGADAH

All say:

בָּרוּךְ אַתָּה ה׳, אֱלֹהֵינוּ מֶלֶךְ הָעוֹלָם, הַזָּן אֶת הָעוֹלָם כֻּלּוֹ בְּטוּבוֹ בְּחֵן בְּחֶסֶד וּבְרַחֲמִים, הוּא נוֹתֵן לֶחֶם לְכָל בָּשָׂר כִּי לְעוֹלָם חַסְדּוֹ. וּבְטוּבוֹ הַגָּדוֹל תָּמִיד לֹא חָסַר לָנוּ, וְאַל יֶחְסַר לָנוּ מָזוֹן לְעוֹלָם וָעֶד. בַּעֲבוּר שְׁמוֹ הַגָּדוֹל, כִּי הוּא אֵל זָן וּמְפַרְנֵס לַכֹּל וּמֵטִיב לַכֹּל, וּמֵכִין מָזוֹן לְכָל בְּרִיּוֹתָיו אֲשֶׁר בָּרָא. בָּרוּךְ אַתָּה ה׳, הַזָּן אֶת הַכֹּל.

נוֹדֶה לְךָ ה׳ אֱלֹהֵינוּ עַל שֶׁהִנְחַלְתָּ לַאֲבוֹתֵינוּ אֶרֶץ חֶמְדָּה טוֹבָה וּרְחָבָה, וְעַל שֶׁהוֹצֵאתָנוּ ה׳ אֱלֹהֵינוּ מֵאֶרֶץ מִצְרַיִם, וּפְדִיתָנוּ מִבֵּית עֲבָדִים, וְעַל בְּרִיתְךָ שֶׁחָתַמְתָּ בִּבְשָׂרֵנוּ, וְעַל תּוֹרָתְךָ שֶׁלִּמַּדְתָּנוּ, וְעַל חֻקֶּיךָ שֶׁהוֹדַעְתָּנוּ, וְעַל חַיִּים חֵן וָחֶסֶד שֶׁחוֹנַנְתָּנוּ,

בִּי בָּה דוּ דוּם דוּם, בּוּם בַּדוּם בּוּם בָּן, בָּה דוּ, בָּה דָה דוּם דוּם, דוּם דַּדוּם דוּם דוּם דוּם דוּם. בָּדָה דוּ דוּם דֻּדוּם.

something you do and Divine Grace is something you acquire. Our liturgy appeals directly to God's Grace, not assuming that it always exists within us. The Sages in the Talmud assert that if one gives grace to their fellow people they are given grace from the Almighty. When we engage with the world we interact with Grace, and most clearly with the Grace after Meals. We are thankful for the ability to eat well and pray that will continue. Therefore, Mr Pitt is right. Elaine does carry some grace because she is nice and playful with him. Grace is the way she acts and not some quality she exhibits. During the Seder, it is important to explicitly exhibit Grace. While praying for a future deliverance, receiving Divine Grace is more needed than ever.

and for Your covenant which You have sealed in our flesh, and for Your Torah that You have taught us, and for Your statutes which You have made known to us, and for life, grace and kindness that You have granted us and for the eating of nourishment that You feed and provide for us always, on all days, and at all times and in every hour. And for everything, Lord our God, we thank You, and bless You. May Your name be blessed in the mouths of all living things, always and forever. As it is written, "You will eat and be satisfied and then you will bless Lord your God, for the good land which He has given to you." (Deuteronomy 8:10) Blessed are You, Lord, for the land and for the food.

Please have mercy, Lord our God, upon Israel, Your people; and upon Jerusalem, Your city; and upon Zion, the dwelling place of Your Glory; and upon the monarchy of the House of David, Your appointed one; and upon the great and holy house that Your name is called upon. Our God, our Father, tend us, sustain us, provide for us, relieve us and give us quick relief, Lord our God, from all of our troubles. And please do not make us needy, Lord our God, not for the gifts of flesh and blood, and not for their loans, but rather from Your full, open, holy and broad hand, so that we not be embarrassed and we not be ashamed forever and always.

On Saturday night, add the following paragraph:
May You be pleased to embolden us, Lord our God, in your commandments and in the command of the seventh day, of this great and holy Shabbat, since this day is great and holy before You, to cease work upon it and to rest upon it, with love, according to the commandment of Your will. And with Your will, allow us, Lord our

וְעַל אֲכִילַת מָזוֹן שָׁאַתָּה זָן וּמְפַרְנֵס אוֹתָנוּ תָּמִיד, בְּכָל יוֹם וּבְכָל עֵת וּבְכָל שָׁעָה. וְעַל הַכֹּל ה' אֱלֹהֵינוּ, אֲנַחְנוּ מוֹדִים לָךְ וּמְבָרְכִים אוֹתָךְ, יִתְבָּרַךְ שִׁמְךָ בְּפִי כָּל חַי תָּמִיד לְעוֹלָם וָעֶד. כַּכָּתוּב (דברים ח, י): "וְאָכַלְתָּ וְשָׂבָעְתָּ וּבֵרַכְתָּ אֶת ה' אֱלֹהֶיךָ עַל הָאָרֶץ הַטֹּבָה אֲשֶׁר נָתַן לָךְ." בָּרוּךְ אַתָּה ה', עַל הָאָרֶץ וְעַל הַמָּזוֹן.

רַחֵם נָא ה' אֱלֹהֵינוּ עַל יִשְׂרָאֵל עַמֶּךָ וְעַל יְרוּשָׁלַיִם עִירֶךָ וְעַל צִיּוֹן מִשְׁכַּן כְּבוֹדֶךָ וְעַל מַלְכוּת בֵּית דָּוִד מְשִׁיחֶךָ וְעַל הַבַּיִת הַגָּדוֹל וְהַקָּדוֹשׁ שֶׁנִּקְרָא שִׁמְךָ עָלָיו. אֱלֹהֵינוּ אָבִינוּ, רְעֵנוּ זוּנֵנוּ פַּרְנְסֵנוּ וְכַלְכְּלֵנוּ וְהַרְוִיחֵנוּ, וְהַרְוַח לָנוּ ה' אֱלֹהֵינוּ מְהֵרָה מִכָּל צָרוֹתֵינוּ. וְנָא אַל תַּצְרִיכֵנוּ ה' אֱלֹהֵינוּ, לֹא לִידֵי מַתְּנַת בָּשָׂר וָדָם וְלֹא לִידֵי הַלְוָאָתָם, כִּי אִם לְיָדְךָ הַמְּלֵאָה הַפְּתוּחָה הַקְּדוֹשָׁה וְהָרְחָבָה, שֶׁלֹּא נֵבוֹשׁ וְלֹא נִכָּלֵם לְעוֹלָם וָעֶד.

On Saturday night, add the following paragraph:

רְצֵה וְהַחֲלִיצֵנוּ ה' אֱלֹהֵינוּ בְּמִצְוֹתֶיךָ וּבְמִצְוַת יוֹם הַשְּׁבִיעִי הַשַּׁבָּת הַגָּדוֹל וְהַקָּדוֹשׁ הַזֶּה. כִּי יוֹם זֶה גָּדוֹל וְקָדוֹשׁ הוּא לְפָנֶיךָ לִשְׁבָּת בּוֹ וְלָנוּחַ בּוֹ בְּאַהֲבָה כְּמִצְוַת רְצוֹנֶךָ. וּבִרְצוֹנְךָ

God, that we should not have trouble, and grief and sighing on the day of our rest. And may You show us, Lord our God, the consolation of Zion, Your city and the building of Jerusalem, Your holy city, since You are the Master of salvations and the Master of consolations.

Our God and the God of our forefathers, may there ascend, come, reach, be seen, wanted and heard, remembered and recalled before You, our recollection and remembrance, the remembrance of our forefathers, and the remembrance of the Mashiach, son of David Your servant, and the remembrance of Jerusalem, city of Your holiness, and the remembrance of all Your nation, the house of Israel for deliverance, for good, for grace, for kindness, and for mercy, for life and for peace on this day of the Festival of Matzot. Remember us, Lord our God, on it for good and recall us on it for survival and save us on it for life, and by the word of salvation and mercy, pity and grace us and have mercy on us and save us, since our eyes are upon You, since You are a graceful and merciful Power. And may You build Jerusalem, the holy city, quickly and in our days. Blessed are You, Lord, who builds Jerusalem in His mercy. Amen.

Blessed are You, Lord our God, King of the Universe, God, our Father, our King, our Mightiness, our Creator, our Redeemer, our Maker, our Holy One, the Holy One of Jacob, our Shepherd, the Shepherd of Israel, the King Who is good and beneficent to all, each and every day. He has been beneficent, He is beneficent and He will be beneficent to us. He has bestowed upon us, He bestows upon us and He will bestow upon us forever grace, kindness, mercy; relief, rescue, success; blessing, salvation, consolation; livelihood,

THE (UNOFFICIAL) SEINFELD HAGGADAH

הָנִיחַ לָנוּ ה' אֱלֹהֵינוּ שֶׁלֹּא תְהֵא צָרָה וְיָגוֹן וַאֲנָחָה בְּיוֹם מְנוּחָתֵנוּ. וְהַרְאֵנוּ ה' אֱלֹהֵינוּ בְּנֶחָמַת צִיּוֹן עִירֶךָ וּבְבִנְיַן יְרוּשָׁלַיִם עִיר קָדְשֶׁךָ, כִּי אַתָּה הוּא בַּעַל הַיְשׁוּעוֹת וּבַעַל הַנֶּחָמוֹת.

אֱלֹהֵינוּ וֵאלֹהֵי אֲבוֹתֵינוּ, יַעֲלֶה וְיָבֹא וְיַגִּיעַ וְיֵרָאֶה וְיֵרָצֶה וְיִשָּׁמַע וְיִפָּקֵד וְיִזָּכֵר זִכְרוֹנֵנוּ וּפִקְדוֹנֵנוּ, וְזִכְרוֹן אֲבוֹתֵינוּ, וְזִכְרוֹן מָשִׁיחַ בֶּן דָּוִד עַבְדֶּךָ, וְזִכְרוֹן יְרוּשָׁלַיִם עִיר קָדְשֶׁךָ, וְזִכְרוֹן כָּל עַמְּךָ בֵּית יִשְׂרָאֵל לְפָנֶיךָ, לִפְלֵיטָה לְטוֹבָה לְחֵן וּלְחֶסֶד וּלְרַחֲמִים, לְחַיִּים וּלְשָׁלוֹם בְּיוֹם חַג הַמַּצּוֹת הַזֶּה. זָכְרֵנוּ ה' אֱלֹהֵינוּ בּוֹ לְטוֹבָה, וּפָקְדֵנוּ בוֹ לִבְרָכָה, וְהוֹשִׁיעֵנוּ בוֹ לְחַיִּים. וּבִדְבַר יְשׁוּעָה וְרַחֲמִים, חוּס וְחָנֵּנוּ וְרַחֵם עָלֵינוּ וְהוֹשִׁיעֵנוּ, כִּי אֵלֶיךָ עֵינֵינוּ, כִּי אֵל מֶלֶךְ חַנּוּן וְרַחוּם אָתָּה. וּבְנֵה יְרוּשָׁלַיִם עִיר הַקֹּדֶשׁ בִּמְהֵרָה בְיָמֵינוּ. בָּרוּךְ אַתָּה ה', בּוֹנֵה בְרַחֲמָיו יְרוּשָׁלָיִם. אָמֵן.

בָּרוּךְ אַתָּה ה', אֱלֹהֵינוּ מֶלֶךְ הָעוֹלָם, הָאֵל אָבִינוּ מַלְכֵּנוּ אַדִּירֵנוּ בּוֹרְאֵנוּ גּוֹאֲלֵנוּ יוֹצְרֵנוּ קְדוֹשֵׁנוּ קְדוֹשׁ יַעֲקֹב רוֹעֵנוּ רוֹעֵה יִשְׂרָאֵל הַמֶּלֶךְ הַטּוֹב וְהַמֵּטִיב לַכֹּל שֶׁבְּכָל יוֹם וָיוֹם הוּא הֵטִיב, הוּא מֵטִיב, הוּא יֵיטִיב לָנוּ. הוּא גְמָלָנוּ הוּא גוֹמְלֵנוּ הוּא יִגְמְלֵנוּ לָעַד, לְחֵן וּלְחֶסֶד וּלְרַחֲמִים וּלְרֶוַח הַצָּלָה וְהַצְלָחָה, בְּרָכָה וִישׁוּעָה נֶחָמָה פַּרְנָסָה וְכַלְכָּלָה וְרַחֲמִים וְחַיִּים

ברך – 117

sustenance, life, peace and all good. May He never cause us to lack anything good.

May the Merciful One reign over us forever and always.
May the Merciful One be blessed in the heavens and in the earth.
May the Merciful One be praised for all generations, and exalted among us forever and ever, and glorified among us always and infinitely for all infinities.
May the Merciful One sustain us honorably.
May the Merciful One break our yolk from upon our necks and bring us upright to our land.
May the Merciful One send us multiple blessings, to this home and upon this table upon which we have eaten.
May the Merciful One send us Eliyahu the prophet - may he be remembered for good - and he shall announce to us tidings of good, of salvation and of consolation.
May the Merciful One bless my [husband/my wife,] [my father, my teacher,] the master of this home and [my mother, my teacher,] the mistress of this home, they and their home and their offspring and everything that is theirs, us and all that is ours; as were blessed Avraham, Yitzchak and Yaakov, in everything, from everything, with everything, so too should He bless us, all of us together, with a complete blessing and we shall say, Amen.

From above, may they advocate upon them and upon us merit, that should protect us in peace; and may we carry a blessing from the Lord and charity from the God of our salvation; and find grace and good understanding in the eyes of God and man.

THE (UNOFFICIAL) SEINFELD HAGGADAH

וְשָׁלוֹם וְכָל טוֹב, וּמִכָּל טוֹב לְעוֹלָם עַל יְחַסְּרֵנוּ.

הָרַחֲמָן הוּא יִמְלוֹךְ עָלֵינוּ לְעוֹלָם וָעֶד.
הָרַחֲמָן הוּא יִתְבָּרַךְ בַּשָּׁמַיִם וּבָאָרֶץ.
הָרַחֲמָן הוּא יִשְׁתַּבַּח לְדוֹר דּוֹרִים, וְיִתְפָּאַר בָּנוּ לָעַד וּלְנֵצַח נְצָחִים, וְיִתְהַדַּר בָּנוּ לָעַד וּלְעוֹלְמֵי עוֹלָמִים.
הָרַחֲמָן הוּא יְפַרְנְסֵנוּ בְּכָבוֹד.
הָרַחֲמָן הוּא יִשְׁבּוֹר עֻלֵּנוּ מֵעַל צַוָּארֵנוּ, וְהוּא יוֹלִיכֵנוּ קוֹמְמִיּוּת לְאַרְצֵנוּ.
הָרַחֲמָן הוּא יִשְׁלַח לָנוּ בְּרָכָה מְרֻבָּה בַּבַּיִת הַזֶּה, וְעַל שֻׁלְחָן זֶה שֶׁאָכַלְנוּ עָלָיו.
הָרַחֲמָן הוּא יִשְׁלַח לָנוּ אֶת אֵלִיָּהוּ הַנָּבִיא זָכוּר לַטּוֹב, וִיבַשֶּׂר לָנוּ בְּשׂוֹרוֹת טוֹבוֹת יְשׁוּעוֹת וְנֶחָמוֹת.
הָרַחֲמָן הוּא יְבָרֵךְ אֶת [בַּעֲלִי/אִשְׁתִּי,] [אָבִי מוֹרִי] בַּעַל הַבַּיִת הַזֶּה, וְאֶת [אִמִּי מוֹרָתִי] בַּעֲלַת הַבַּיִת הַזֶּה, אוֹתָם וְאֶת בֵּיתָם וְאֶת זַרְעָם וְאֶת כָּל אֲשֶׁר לָהֶם, אוֹתָנוּ וְאֶת כָּל אֲשֶׁר לָנוּ, כְּמוֹ שֶׁנִּתְבָּרְכוּ אֲבוֹתֵינוּ אַבְרָהָם יִצְחָק וְיַעֲקֹב בַּכֹּל מִכֹּל כֹּל, כֵּן יְבָרֵךְ אוֹתָנוּ כֻּלָּנוּ יַחַד בִּבְרָכָה שְׁלֵמָה, וְנֹאמַר, אָמֵן.

בַּמָּרוֹם יְלַמְּדוּ עֲלֵיהֶם וְעָלֵינוּ זְכוּת שֶׁתְּהֵא לְמִשְׁמֶרֶת שָׁלוֹם. וְנִשָּׂא בְרָכָה מֵאֵת ה', וּצְדָקָה מֵאֱלֹהֵי יִשְׁעֵנוּ, וְנִמְצָא חֵן וְשֵׂכֶל טוֹב בְּעֵינֵי אֱלֹהִים וְאָדָם.

THE HAGGADAH ABOUT NOTHING

[On Shabbat, we say: May the Merciful One give us to inherit the day that will be completely Shabbat and rest in everlasting life.]

May the Merciful One give us to inherit the day that will be all good. [The day that is all long, the day that the righteous will sit and their crowns will be on their heads and they will enjoy the radiance of the Divine presence and our share be with them.]

May the Merciful One give us merit for the times of the messiah and for life in the world to come. A tower of salvations is our King; may He do kindness with his messiah, with David and his offspring, forever (II Samuel 22:51). The One who makes peace above, may He make peace upon us and upon all of Israel; and say, Amen.

Fear the Lord, His holy ones, since there is no lacking for those that fear Him. Young lions may go without hunger, but those that seek the Lord will not lack any good thing (Psalms 34:10-11). Thank the Lord, since He is good, since His kindness is forever (Psalms 118:1). You open Your hand and satisfy the will of all living things (Psalms 146:16). Blessed is the man that trusts in the Lord and the Lord is his security (Jeremiah 17:7). I was a youth and I have also aged and I have not seen a righteous man forsaken and his offspring seeking bread (Psalms 37:25). The Lord will give courage to His people. The Lord will bless His people with peace (Psalms 29:11).

[בשבת: הָרַחֲמָן הוּא יַנְחִילֵנוּ יוֹם שֶׁכֻּלּוֹ שַׁבָּת וּמְנוּחָה לְחַיֵּי הָעוֹלָמִים.]

הָרַחֲמָן הוּא יַנְחִילֵנוּ יוֹם שֶׁכֻּלּוֹ טוֹב. [יוֹם שֶׁכֻּלּוֹ אָרוּךְ. יוֹם שֶׁצַּדִּיקִים יוֹשְׁבִים וְעַטְרוֹתֵיהֶם בְּרָאשֵׁיהֶם וְנֶהֱנִים מִזִּיו הַשְּׁכִינָה וִיהִי חֶלְקֵנוּ עִמָּהֶם.]

הָרַחֲמָן הוּא יְזַכֵּנוּ לִימוֹת הַמָּשִׁיחַ וּלְחַיֵּי הָעוֹלָם הַבָּא.

מִגְדּוֹל יְשׁוּעוֹת מַלְכּוֹ וְעֹשֶׂה חֶסֶד לִמְשִׁיחוֹ לְדָוִד וּלְזַרְעוֹ עַד עוֹלָם (שמואל ב' כב, נא). עֹשֶׂה שָׁלוֹם בִּמְרוֹמָיו, הוּא יַעֲשֶׂה שָׁלוֹם עָלֵינוּ וְעַל כָּל יִשְׂרָאֵל; וְאִמְרוּ, אָמֵן.

יְראוּ אֶת ה' קְדֹשָׁיו, כִּי אֵין מַחְסוֹר לִירֵאָיו. כְּפִירִים רָשׁוּ וְרָעֵבוּ, וְדֹרְשֵׁי ה' לֹא יַחְסְרוּ כָל טוֹב (תהלים לד, ט-י). הוֹדוּ לַה' כִּי טוֹב כִּי לְעוֹלָם חַסְדּוֹ (תהלים קיח, א). פּוֹתֵחַ אֶת יָדֶךָ, וּמַשְׂבִּיעַ לְכָל חַי רָצוֹן (תהלים קמה, טז). בָּרוּךְ הַגֶּבֶר אֲשֶׁר יִבְטַח בַּה', וְהָיָה ה' מִבְטַחוֹ (ירמיהו יז, ז). נַעַר הָיִיתִי גַּם זָקַנְתִּי, וְלֹא רָאִיתִי צַדִּיק נֶעֱזָב, וְזַרְעוֹ מְבַקֶּשׁ לָחֶם (תהלים לז, כה). ה' עֹז לְעַמּוֹ יִתֵּן, ה' יְבָרֵךְ אֶת עַמּוֹ בַשָּׁלוֹם (תהלים כט, יא).

THE HAGGADAH ABOUT NOTHING

THIRD CUP OF WINE

Raise the cup and say:

Blessed are You, Lord our God, King of the universe, who creates the fruit of the vine.

We drink while reclining and do not say a blessing afterwards.

POUR OUT THY WRATH

We pour the cup of Eliyahu and open the door. Hopefully the lighting on the porch is good[78].

Pour your wrath upon the nations that do not know You and upon the kingdoms that do not call upon Your Name! For they have devoured Yaakov and laid waste his habitation (Psalms 79:6-7). Pour out Your fury upon them and let your fierce anger overtake them, like an old man trying to send back soup at a deli[79] (Psalms 69:25)! Pursue them with anger and eradicate them from beneath the heavens of the Lord (Lamentations 3:66).

BEE BA DO DUM DUM, BUM BADUM BUM BUH, BAH DUH, BAH DAH DUM DUM, DUM DEDUM DUM DUM DUM DUM. BADA DO DUM DEDUM.

The Real Pop in Guy

Jerry would probably hate Eliyahu, who visits every home on the Seder night. He's too much of a pop in guy.

The Vengeance of Newman

This paragraph in the Haggadah can be difficult with modern sensibilities, but would probably make sense to Newman. How can we ask God to pour out His wrath on those that oppose Him. Should we not be asking for mercy? Rabbi Yaakov Glasser, current Dean of the CJF at Yeshiva University and my former NCSY Regional Director, notes that after a full night of remembering past oppressions, and hoping for reprieve from more modern ones, it would be natural to

THE (UNOFFICIAL) SEINFELD HAGGADAH

כוס שלישית

Raise the cup and say:

בָּרוּךְ אַתָּה ה', אֱלֹהֵינוּ מֶלֶךְ הָעוֹלָם, בּוֹרֵא פְּרִי הַגָּפֶן.

We drink while reclining and do not say a blessing afterwards.

[NEW YORK GLASSMAN license plate]

שפוך חמתך

We pour the cup of Eliyahu and open the door. Hopefully the lighting on the porch is good.

שְׁפֹךְ חֲמָתְךָ אֶל־הַגּוֹיִם אֲשֶׁר לֹא יְדָעוּךָ וְעַל־מַמְלָכוֹת אֲשֶׁר בְּשִׁמְךָ לֹא קָרָאוּ. כִּי אָכַל אֶת־יַעֲקֹב וְאֶת־נָוֵהוּ הֵשַׁמּוּ (תהלים עט, ו-ז). שְׁפָךְ־עֲלֵיהֶם זַעְמֶךָ וַחֲרוֹן אַפְּךָ יַשִּׂיגֵם (תהלים סט, כה). תִּרְדֹּף בְּאַף וְתַשְׁמִידֵם מִתַּחַת שְׁמֵי ה' (איכה ג, סו).

=== בי בה דו דום דום, בום בדום בום בו, בה דו, בה דה דום דום, דום דדום דום דום דום, בדה דו דום דדום. ===

want some wrath poured. The Haggadah has us ask God to do this before Hallel so that we can believe that God has a path of history. We can only give up our want for revenge because we believe God is taking care of His vengeance.

    In the everlasting battle between Jerry and Newman, only Jerry has this attitude. Even though Jerry really despises Newman, he never tries to affront Newman. Jerry tries to catch Newman in his lies, but never goes out of his way to actually harm him. Jerry lets Newman fail on his own by tempting him (usually with snacks), but never tries to pour his wrath on him. Conversely, Newman does try to catch Jerry. In "The Package[C149]," Newman goes to great lengths to try and trap Jerry for him to pay penance. He is similarly overjoyed when they are on trial in the Finale. In "The Millenium[C150]," he argues with Kramer over inviting Jerry to their co-hosted millennium party saying that "For me, the next millennium must be Jerry free." If only Newman could go to a Seder to learn not to exact revenge.

Hallel

SECOND HALF OF HALLEL

We pour the fourth cup and complete the Hallel.

Not to us, not to us, but rather to Your name, give glory for your kindness and for your truth. Why should the nations say, "Say, where is their God?" But our God is in the heavens, all that He wanted, He has done. Their idols are silver and gold, the work of men's hands. They have a mouth but do not speak; they have eyes but do not see. They have ears but do not hear; they have a nose but do not smell; hands, but they do not feel; feet, but do not walk; they do not make a peep from their throat. Like them will be their makers, all those that trust in them. Israel, trust in the Lord; their help and shield is He. House of Aharon, trust in the Lord; their help and shield is He. Those that fear the Lord, trust in the Lord; their help and shield is He. (Psalms 115:1-11)

The Lord who remembers us, will bless; He will bless the House of Israel; He will bless the House of Aharon. He will bless those that fear the Lord, the small ones with the great ones. May the Lord bring increase to you, to you and to your children. Blessed are you to the Lord, the maker of the heavens and the earth. The heavens are the Lord's heavens, but the earth He has given to the children of man. It is not the dead that will praise the Lord, and not those that go down

הלל

חצי שני של הלל

We pour the fourth cup and complete the Hallel.

לֹא לָנוּ, ה', לֹא לָנוּ, כִּי לְשִׁמְךָ תֵּן כָּבוֹד, עַל חַסְדְּךָ עַל אֲמִתֶּךָ. לָמָּה יֹאמְרוּ הַגּוֹיִם אַיֵּה נָא אֱלֹהֵיהֶם. וֵאלֹהֵינוּ בַשָּׁמָיִם, כֹּל אֲשֶׁר חָפֵץ עָשָׂה. עֲצַבֵּיהֶם כֶּסֶף וְזָהָב מַעֲשֵׂה יְדֵי אָדָם. פֶּה לָהֶם וְלֹא יְדַבֵּרוּ, עֵינַיִם לָהֶם וְלֹא יִרְאוּ. אָזְנַיִם לָהֶם וְלֹא יִשְׁמָעוּ, אַף לָהֶם וְלֹא יְרִיחוּן. יְדֵיהֶם וְלֹא יְמִישׁוּן, רַגְלֵיהֶם וְלֹא יְהַלֵּכוּ, לֹא יֶהְגּוּ בִּגְרוֹנָם. כְּמוֹהֶם יִהְיוּ עֹשֵׂיהֶם, כֹּל אֲשֶׁר בֹּטֵחַ בָּהֶם. יִשְׂרָאֵל בְּטַח בַּה', עֶזְרָם וּמָגִנָּם הוּא. בֵּית אַהֲרֹן בִּטְחוּ בַה', עֶזְרָם וּמָגִנָּם הוּא. יִרְאֵי ה' בִּטְחוּ בַה', עֶזְרָם וּמָגִנָּם הוּא! (תהלים קטו, א-יא)

ה' זְכָרָנוּ יְבָרֵךְ. יְבָרֵךְ אֶת בֵּית יִשְׂרָאֵל, יְבָרֵךְ אֶת בֵּית אַהֲרֹן, יְבָרֵךְ יִרְאֵי ה', הַקְּטַנִּים עִם הַגְּדֹלִים. יֹסֵף ה' עֲלֵיכֶם, עֲלֵיכֶם וְעַל בְּנֵיכֶם. בְּרוּכִים אַתֶּם לַה', עֹשֵׂה שָׁמַיִם וָאָרֶץ. הַשָּׁמַיִם שָׁמַיִם לַה' וְהָאָרֶץ נָתַן לִבְנֵי אָדָם. לֹא הַמֵּתִים יְהַלְלוּ יָהּ וְלֹא כָּל יֹרְדֵי

to silence. But we will bless the Lord from now and forever. Halleluyah! (Psalms 115:12-18)

I have loved the Lord - since He hears my voice, my supplications. Since He inclined His ear to me - and in my days, I will call out. The pangs of death have encircled me and the straits of the Pit have found me and I found grief. And in the name of the Lord I called, "Please Lord, Spare my soul." Gracious is the Lord and righteous, and our God acts mercifully. The Lord watches over the silly; I was poor and He has saved me. Return, my soul to your tranquility, since the Lord has favored you. Since You have rescued my soul from death, my eyes from tears, my feet from stumbling. I will walk before the Lord in the lands of the living. I have trusted, when I speak - I am very afflicted. I said in my haste, all men are hypocritical. (Psalms 116:1-11)

What can I give back to the Lord for all that He has favored me? A cup of salvations I will raise up and I will call out in the name of the Lord. My vows to the Lord I will pay, now in front of His entire people. Precious in the eyes of the Lord is the death of His pious ones. Please Lord, since I am Your servant, the son of Your maidservant; You have opened my chains. To You will I offer a thanksgiving offering and I will call out in the name of the Lord. My vows to the Lord I will pay, now in front of His entire people. In the courtyards of the house of the Lord, in your midst, Jerusalem. Halleluyah! (Psalms 116:12-19)

דוּמָה. וַאֲנַחְנוּ נְבָרֵךְ יָהּ מֵעַתָּה וְעַד עוֹלָם. הַלְלוּיָהּ!

(תהלים קטו, יב-יח)

אָהַבְתִּי כִּי יִשְׁמַע ה' אֶת קוֹלִי תַּחֲנוּנָי. כִּי הִטָּה אָזְנוֹ לִי וּבְיָמַי אֶקְרָא. אֲפָפוּנִי חֶבְלֵי מָוֶת וּמְצָרֵי שְׁאוֹל מְצָאוּנִי, צָרָה וְיָגוֹן אֶמְצָא. וּבְשֵׁם ה' אֶקְרָא: אָנָּא ה' מַלְּטָה נַפְשִׁי. חַנּוּן ה' וְצַדִּיק, וֵאלֹהֵינוּ מְרַחֵם. שֹׁמֵר פְּתָאִים ה', דַּלּוֹתִי וְלִי יְהוֹשִׁיעַ. שׁוּבִי נַפְשִׁי לִמְנוּחָיְכִי, כִּי ה' גָּמַל עָלָיְכִי. כִּי חִלַּצְתָּ נַפְשִׁי מִמָּוֶת, אֶת עֵינִי מִן דִּמְעָה, אֶת רַגְלִי מִדֶּחִי. אֶתְהַלֵּךְ לִפְנֵי ה' בְּאַרְצוֹת הַחַיִּים. הֶאֱמַנְתִּי כִּי אֲדַבֵּר, אֲנִי עָנִיתִי מְאֹד. אֲנִי אָמַרְתִּי בְחָפְזִי כָּל הָאָדָם כֹּזֵב.

(תהלים קטז, א-יא)

מָה אָשִׁיב לַה' כֹּל תַּגְמוּלוֹהִי עָלָי. כּוֹס יְשׁוּעוֹת אֶשָּׂא וּבְשֵׁם ה' אֶקְרָא. נְדָרַי לַה' אֲשַׁלֵּם נֶגְדָה נָּא לְכָל עַמּוֹ. יָקָר בְּעֵינֵי ה' הַמָּוְתָה לַחֲסִידָיו. אָנָּה ה' כִּי אֲנִי עַבְדֶּךָ, אֲנִי עַבְדְּךָ בֶּן אֲמָתֶךָ, פִּתַּחְתָּ לְמוֹסֵרָי. לְךָ אֶזְבַּח זֶבַח תּוֹדָה וּבְשֵׁם ה' אֶקְרָא. נְדָרַי לַה' אֲשַׁלֵּם נֶגְדָה נָּא לְכָל עַמּוֹ. בְּחַצְרוֹת בֵּית ה', בְּתוֹכֵכִי יְרוּשָׁלָיִם. הַלְלוּיָהּ! (תהלים קטז, יב-יט)

Praise the name of the Lord, all nations; extol Him all peoples. When people will look to the (black and white) cookie, all our problems would be solved[80]. Since His kindness has overwhelmed us and the truth of the Lord is forever. Halleluyah! (Psalm 117)

Thank the Lord, since He is good, since His kindness is forever. Let Israel now say, "Thank the Lord, since He is good, since His kindness is forever." Let the House of Aharon now say, "Thank the Lord, since He is good, since His kindness is forever." Let those that fear the Lord now say, "Thank the Lord, since He is good, since His kindness is forever." (Psalms 118:1-4)

From the strait I have called, Lord; He answered me from the wide space, the Lord. The Lord is for me, I will not fear, what will man do to me? The Lord is for me with my helpers, and I shall glare at those that hate me. It is better to take refuge with the Lord than to trust in man. It is better to take refuge with the Lord than to trust in nobles. All the nations surrounded me - in the name of the Lord, as I will chop them off. They surrounded me, they also encircled me - in the name of the Lord, as I will chop them off. They surrounded me like bees, they were extinguished like a fire of thorns - in the name of the Lord, as I will chop them off. You have surely pushed me to fall, but the Lord helped me. My boldness and song is the Lord, and He has become my salvation. The sound of happy song and salvation is in the tents of the righteous, the right hand of the Lord acts powerfully. I will not die but rather I will live and tell over the acts of the Lord. The Lord has surely chastised me, but He has not given me over to death. Open

THE (UNOFFICIAL) SEINFELD HAGGADAH

הַלְלוּ אֶת ה' כָּל גּוֹיִם, שַׁבְּחוּהוּ כָּל הָאֻמִּים. כִּי גָבַר עָלֵינוּ חַסְדּוֹ, וֶאֱמֶת ה' לְעוֹלָם. הַלְלוּיָהּ.
(תהלים קיז)

הוֹדוּ לַה' כִּי טוֹב	כִּי לְעוֹלָם חַסְדּוֹ.
יֹאמַר נָא יִשְׂרָאֵל	כִּי לְעוֹלָם חַסְדּוֹ.
יֹאמְרוּ נָא בֵית אַהֲרֹן	כִּי לְעוֹלָם חַסְדּוֹ.
יֹאמְרוּ נָא יִרְאֵי ה'	כִּי לְעוֹלָם חַסְדּוֹ.

(תהלים קיח, א-ד)

מִן הַמֵּצַר קָרָאתִי יָּהּ, עָנָנִי בַמֶּרְחָב יָהּ. ה' לִי, לֹא אִירָא, מַה יַּעֲשֶׂה לִי אָדָם. ה' לִי בְּעֹזְרָי וַאֲנִי אֶרְאֶה בְשֹׂנְאָי. טוֹב לַחֲסוֹת בַּה' מִבְּטֹחַ בָּאָדָם. טוֹב לַחֲסוֹת בַּה' מִבְּטֹחַ בִּנְדִיבִים. כָּל גּוֹיִם סְבָבוּנִי, בְּשֵׁם ה' כִּי אֲמִילַם. סַבּוּנִי גַם סְבָבוּנִי, בְּשֵׁם ה' כִּי אֲמִילַם. סַבּוּנִי כִדְבוֹרִים, דֹּעֲכוּ כְּאֵשׁ קוֹצִים, בְּשֵׁם ה' כִּי אֲמִילַם. דָּחֹה דְחִיתַנִי לִנְפֹּל, וַה' עֲזָרָנִי. עָזִּי וְזִמְרָת יָהּ וַיְהִי לִי לִישׁוּעָה. קוֹל רִנָּה וִישׁוּעָה בְּאָהֳלֵי צַדִּיקִים. יְמִין ה' עֹשָׂה חָיִל, יְמִין ה' רוֹמֵמָה, יְמִין ה' עֹשָׂה חָיִל. לֹא אָמוּת כִּי אֶחְיֶה, וַאֲסַפֵּר מַעֲשֵׂי יָהּ. יַסֹּר יִסְּרַנִּי יָּהּ, וְלַמָּוֶת לֹא נְתָנָנִי. פִּתְחוּ לִי שַׁעֲרֵי צֶדֶק, אָבֹא בָם, אוֹדֶה יָהּ. זֶה הַשַּׁעַר לַה', צַדִּיקִים יָבֹאוּ בוֹ. אוֹדְךָ כִּי עֲנִיתָנִי וַתְּהִי לִי לִישׁוּעָה. (אוֹדְךָ כִּי עֲנִיתָנִי וַתְּהִי לִי לִישׁוּעָה. אֶבֶן

up for me the gates of righteousness; I will enter them, thank the Lord. This is the gate of the Lord, the righteous will enter it. I will thank You, since You answered me and You have become my salvation. The stone that was left by the builders has become the main cornerstone. From the Lord was this, it is wondrous in our eyes. This is the day of the Lord, let us exult and rejoice upon it. (Psalms 118:5-24)

> Please, Lord, save us now;
> Please, Lord, save us now!
> Please, Lord, give us success now;
> Please, Lord, give us success now! (Psalms 118:25)

Blessed be the one who comes in the name of the Lord, we have blessed you from the house of the Lord. God is the Lord, and He has illuminated us; tie up the festival offering with ropes until it reaches the corners of the altar. You are my Power and I will Thank You; my God and I will exalt You. Thank the Lord, since He is good, since His kindness is forever.(Psalms 118:26-29)

All of your works shall praise You, Lord our God, and your pious ones, the righteous ones who do Your will; and all of Your people, the House of Israel will thank and bless in joyful song: and extol and glorify, and exalt and acclaim, and sanctify and coronate Your name, our King. Since, You it is good to thank, and to Your name it is pleasant to sing, since from always and forever are you the Power.

מָאֲסוּ הַבּוֹנִים הָיְתָה לְרֹאשׁ פִּנָּה. אֶבֶן מָאֲסוּ הַבּוֹנִים הָיְתָה לְרֹאשׁ פִּנָּה. מֵאֵת ה' הָיְתָה זֹּאת הִיא נִפְלָאת בְּעֵינֵינוּ. מֵאֵת ה' הָיְתָה זֹּאת הִיא נִפְלָאת בְּעֵינֵינוּ. זֶה הַיּוֹם עָשָׂה ה'. נָגִילָה וְנִשְׂמְחָה בוֹ. זֶה הַיּוֹם עָשָׂה ה'. נָגִילָה וְנִשְׂמְחָה בוֹ. (תהלים קיח, ה-כד)

אָנָּא ה', הוֹשִׁיעָה נָּא.
אָנָּא ה', הוֹשִׁיעָה נָּא.
אָנָּא ה', הַצְלִיחָה נָא.
אָנָּא ה', הַצְלִיחָה נָא. (תהלים קיח, כה)

בָּרוּךְ הַבָּא בְּשֵׁם ה', בֵּרַכְנוּכֶם מִבֵּית ה'. בָּרוּךְ הַבָּא בְּשֵׁם ה', בֵּרַכְנוּכֶם מִבֵּית ה'. אֵל ה' וַיָּאֶר לָנוּ. אִסְרוּ חַג בַּעֲבֹתִים עַד קַרְנוֹת הַמִּזְבֵּחַ. אֵל ה' וַיָּאֶר לָנוּ. אִסְרוּ חַג בַּעֲבֹתִים עַד קַרְנוֹת הַמִּזְבֵּחַ. אֵלִי אַתָּה וְאוֹדֶךָּ, אֱלֹהַי, אֲרוֹמְמֶךָּ. אֵלִי אַתָּה וְאוֹדֶךָּ, אֱלֹהַי, אֲרוֹמְמֶךָּ. הוֹדוּ לַה' כִּי טוֹב, כִּי לְעוֹלָם חַסְדּוֹ. הוֹדוּ לַה' כִּי טוֹב, כִּי לְעוֹלָם חַסְדּוֹ. (תהלים קיח, כו-כט)

יְהַלְלוּךָ ה' אֱלֹהֵינוּ כָּל מַעֲשֶׂיךָ, וַחֲסִידֶיךָ צַדִּיקִים עוֹשֵׂי רְצוֹנֶךָ, וְכָל עַמְּךָ בֵּית יִשְׂרָאֵל בְּרִנָּה יוֹדוּ וִיבָרְכוּ, וִישַׁבְּחוּ וִיפָאֲרוּ, וִירוֹמְמוּ וְיַעֲרִיצוּ, וְיַקְדִּישׁוּ וְיַמְלִיכוּ אֶת שִׁמְךָ, מַלְכֵּנוּ. כִּי לְךָ טוֹב לְהוֹדוֹת וּלְשִׁמְךָ נָאֶה לְזַמֵּר, כִּי מֵעוֹלָם וְעַד עוֹלָם אַתָּה אֵל.

SONGS OF PRAISE AND THANKS

Thank the Lord, since He is good, since His kindness is forever. Thank the Power of powers since His kindness is forever. To the Master of masters, since His kindness is forever. To the One who alone does wondrously great deeds, since His kindness is forever. To the one who made the Heavens with discernment, since His kindness is forever. To the One who spread the earth over the waters, since His kindness is forever. To the One who made great lights, since His kindness is forever. The sun to rule in the day, since His kindness is forever. The moon and the stars to rule in the night, since His kindness is forever. To the One that smote Egypt through their firstborn, since His kindness is forever. And He took Israel out from among them, since His kindness is forever. With a strong hand and an outstretched forearm, since His kindness is forever. To the One who cut up the Reed Sea into strips, since His kindness is forever. And He made Israel to pass through it, since His kindness is forever. And He jolted Pharaoh and his troop in the Reed Sea, since His kindness is forever. To the One who led his people in the wilderness, since His kindness is forever. To the One who smote great kings, since His kindness is forever. And he killed mighty kings, since His kindness is forever. Sichon, king of the Amorite, since His kindness is forever. And Og, king of the Bashan, since His kindness is forever. And he gave their land as an inheritance, since His kindness is forever. An inheritance for Israel, His servant, since His kindness is forever. That in our lowliness, He remembered us, since His kindness is forever. And he delivered us from our adversaries, since His kindness

מזמורי הודיה

הוֹדוּ לַיְיָ כִּי טוֹב כִּי לְעוֹלָם חַסְדּוֹ. הוֹדוּ לֵאלֹהֵי הָאֱלֹהִים כִּי לְעוֹלָם חַסְדּוֹ. הוֹדוּ לַאֲדֹנֵי הָאֲדֹנִים כִּי לְעוֹלָם חַסְדּוֹ. לְעֹשֵׂה נִפְלָאוֹת גְּדֹלוֹת לְבַדּוֹ כִּי לְעוֹלָם חַסְדּוֹ. לְעֹשֵׂה הַשָּׁמַיִם בִּתְבוּנָה כִּי לְעוֹלָם חַסְדּוֹ. לְרוֹקַע הָאָרֶץ עַל הַמָּיִם כִּי לְעוֹלָם חַסְדּוֹ. לְעֹשֵׂה אוֹרִים גְּדֹלִים כִּי לְעוֹלָם חַסְדּוֹ. אֶת הַשֶּׁמֶשׁ לְמֶמְשֶׁלֶת בַּיּוֹם כִּי לְעוֹלָם חַסְדּוֹ. אֶת הַיָּרֵחַ וְכוֹכָבִים לְמֶמְשְׁלוֹת בַּלָּיְלָה כִּי לְעוֹלָם חַסְדּוֹ. לְמַכֵּה מִצְרַיִם בִּבְכוֹרֵיהֶם כִּי לְעוֹלָם חַסְדּוֹ. וַיּוֹצֵא יִשְׂרָאֵל מִתּוֹכָם כִּי לְעוֹלָם חַסְדּוֹ. בְּיָד חֲזָקָה וּבִזְרוֹעַ נְטוּיָה כִּי לְעוֹלָם חַסְדּוֹ. לְגֹזֵר יַם סוּף לִגְזָרִים כִּי לְעוֹלָם חַסְדּוֹ. וְהֶעֱבִיר יִשְׂרָאֵל בְּתוֹכוֹ כִּי לְעוֹלָם חַסְדּוֹ. וְנִעֵר פַּרְעֹה וְחֵילוֹ בְיַם סוּף כִּי לְעוֹלָם חַסְדּוֹ. לְמוֹלִיךְ עַמּוֹ בַּמִּדְבָּר כִּי לְעוֹלָם חַסְדּוֹ. לְמַכֵּה מְלָכִים גְּדֹלִים כִּי לְעוֹלָם חַסְדּוֹ. וַיַּהֲרֹג מְלָכִים אַדִּירִים כִּי לְעוֹלָם חַסְדּוֹ. לְסִיחוֹן מֶלֶךְ הָאֱמֹרִי כִּי לְעוֹלָם חַסְדּוֹ. וּלְעוֹג מֶלֶךְ הַבָּשָׁן כִּי לְעוֹלָם חַסְדּוֹ. וְנָתַן אַרְצָם לְנַחֲלָה כִּי לְעוֹלָם חַסְדּוֹ. נַחֲלָה לְיִשְׂרָאֵל עַבְדּוֹ כִּי לְעוֹלָם

is forever. He gives bread to all flesh, since His kindness is forever. Thank the Power of the heavens, since His kindness is forever. (Psalms 136)

The soul of every living being shall bless Your Name, Lord our God; the spirit of all flesh shall glorify and exalt Your remembrance always, our King. From the world and until the world, You are the Power, and other than You we have no king, redeemer, or savior, restorer, rescuer, provider, and merciful one in every time of distress and anguish; we have no king, besides You! God of the first ones and the last ones, God of all creatures, Master of all Generations, Who is praised through a multitude of praises, Who guides His world with kindness and His creatures with mercy. The Lord neither slumbers nor sleeps. He who rouses the sleepers and awakens the dozers; He who makes the mute speak, and frees the captives, and supports the falling, and straightens the bent. We thank You alone. Were our mouth as full of song as the sea, and our tongue as full of joyous song as its multitude of waves, and our lips as full of praise as the breadth of the heavens, and our eyes as sparkling as the sun and the moon, and our hands as outspread as the eagles of the sky and our feet as swift as deers — we still could not thank You sufficiently, Lord our God and God of our ancestors, and to bless Your Name for one thousandth of the thousand of thousands of thousands, and myriad myriads, of goodnesses that You performed for our ancestors and for us. From Egypt, Lord our God, did You redeem us and from the house of slaves You restored us. In famine You nourished us, and in plenty you sustained us. From the sword You saved us, and from plague you spared us;

THE (UNOFFICIAL) SEINFELD HAGGADAH

חַסְדּוֹ. שֶׁבְּשִׁפְלֵנוּ זָכַר לָנוּ כִּי לְעוֹלָם חַסְדּוֹ. וַיִּפְרְקֵנוּ מִצָּרֵינוּ כִּי לְעוֹלָם חַסְדּוֹ. נֹתֵן לֶחֶם לְכָל בָּשָׂר כִּי לְעוֹלָם חַסְדּוֹ. הוֹדוּ לְאֵל הַשָּׁמָיִם כִּי לְעוֹלָם חַסְדּוֹ.

(תהלים קלו)

נִשְׁמַת כָּל חַי תְּבָרֵךְ אֶת שִׁמְךָ, ה' אֱלֹהֵינוּ, וְרוּחַ כָּל בָּשָׂר תְּפָאֵר וּתְרוֹמֵם זִכְרְךָ, מַלְכֵּנוּ, תָּמִיד. מִן הָעוֹלָם וְעַד הָעוֹלָם אַתָּה אֵל, וּמִבַּלְעָדֶיךָ אֵין לָנוּ מֶלֶךְ גּוֹאֵל וּמוֹשִׁיעַ, פּוֹדֶה וּמַצִּיל וּמְפַרְנֵס וּמְרַחֵם בְּכָל עֵת צָרָה וְצוּקָה. אֵין לָנוּ מֶלֶךְ אֶלָּא אַתָּה. אֱלֹהֵי הָרִאשׁוֹנִים וְהָאַחֲרוֹנִים, אֱלוֹהַּ כָּל בְּרִיּוֹת, אֲדוֹן כָּל תּוֹלָדוֹת, הַמְהֻלָּל בְּרֹב הַתִּשְׁבָּחוֹת, הַמְנַהֵג עוֹלָמוֹ בְּחֶסֶד וּבְרִיּוֹתָיו בְּרַחֲמִים. וַה' לֹא יָנוּם וְלֹא יִישָׁן - הַמְעוֹרֵר יְשֵׁנִים וְהַמֵּקִיץ נִרְדָּמִים, וְהַמֵּשִׂיחַ אִלְּמִים וְהַמַּתִּיר אֲסוּרִים וְהַסּוֹמֵךְ נוֹפְלִים וְהַזּוֹקֵף כְּפוּפִים. לְךָ לְבַדְּךָ אֲנַחְנוּ מוֹדִים. אִלּוּ פִינוּ מָלֵא שִׁירָה כַיָּם, וּלְשׁוֹנֵנוּ רִנָּה כַּהֲמוֹן גַּלָּיו, וְשִׂפְתוֹתֵינוּ שֶׁבַח כְּמֶרְחֲבֵי רָקִיעַ, וְעֵינֵינוּ מְאִירוֹת כַּשֶּׁמֶשׁ וְכַיָּרֵחַ, וְיָדֵינוּ פְרוּשׂוֹת כְּנִשְׁרֵי שָׁמַיִם, וְרַגְלֵינוּ קַלּוֹת כָּאַיָּלוֹת - אֵין אֲנַחְנוּ מַסְפִּיקִים לְהוֹדוֹת לְךָ, ה' אֱלֹהֵינוּ וֵאלֹהֵי אֲבוֹתֵינוּ, וּלְבָרֵךְ אֶת שִׁמְךָ עַל אַחַת מֵאֶלֶף, אַלְפֵי אֲלָפִים וְרִבֵּי רְבָבוֹת פְּעָמִים הַטּוֹבוֹת שֶׁעָשִׂיתָ עִם אֲבוֹתֵינוּ וְעִמָּנוּ. מִמִּצְרַיִם גְּאַלְתָּנוּ, ה' אֱלֹהֵינוּ, וּמִבֵּית עֲבָדִים פְּדִיתָנוּ,

הלל — 135

and from severe and enduring diseases You delivered us. Until now Your mercy has helped us, and Your kindness has not forsaken us; and do not abandon us, Lord our God, forever. Therefore, the limbs that You set within us and the spirit and soul that You breathed into our nostrils, and the tongue that You placed in our mouth - verily, they shall thank and bless and praise and glorify, and exalt and revere, and sanctify and coronate Your name, our King. For every mouth shall offer thanks to You; and every tongue shall swear allegiance to You; and every knee shall bend to You; and every upright one shall prostrate himself before You; all hearts shall fear You; and all innermost feelings and thoughts shall sing praises to Your name, as the matter is written (Psalms 35:10), "All my bones shall say, 'Lord, who is like You? You save the poor man from one who is stronger than he, the poor and destitute from the one who would rob him.'" Who is similar to You and who is equal to You and who can be compared to You, O great, strong and awesome Power, O highest Power, Creator of the heavens and the earth? We shall praise and extol and glorify and bless Your holy name, as it is stated (Psalms 103:1), "[A Psalm] of David. Bless the Lord, O my soul; and all that is within me, His holy name."

The Power, in Your powerful boldness; the Great, in the glory of Your name; the Strong One forever; the King who sits on His high and elevated throne.

He who dwells always; lofty and holy is His name. And as it is written (Psalms 33:10), "Sing joyfully to the Lord, righteous ones, praise is beautiful from the upright." By the mouth of

THE (UNOFFICIAL) SEINFELD HAGGADAH

בָּרָעָב זַנְתָּנוּ וּבְשָׂבָע כִּלְכַּלְתָּנוּ, מֵחֶרֶב הִצַּלְתָּנוּ וּמִדֶּבֶר מִלַּטְתָּנוּ, וּמֵחֳלָיִם רָעִים וְנֶאֱמָנִים דִּלִּיתָנוּ. עַד הֵנָּה עֲזָרוּנוּ רַחֲמֶיךָ וְלֹא עֲזָבוּנוּ חֲסָדֶיךָ, וְאַל תִּטְּשֵׁנוּ, ה' אֱלֹהֵינוּ, לָנֶצַח. עַל כֵּן אֵבָרִים שֶׁפִּלַּגְתָּ בָּנוּ וְרוּחַ וּנְשָׁמָה שֶׁנָּפַחְתָּ בְּאַפֵּינוּ וְלָשׁוֹן אֲשֶׁר שַׂמְתָּ בְּפִינוּ – הֵן הֵם יוֹדוּ וִיבָרְכוּ וִישַׁבְּחוּ וִיפָאֲרוּ וִירוֹמְמוּ וְיַעֲרִיצוּ וְיַקְדִּישׁוּ וְיַמְלִיכוּ אֶת שִׁמְךָ מַלְכֵּנוּ. כִּי כָל פֶּה לְךָ יוֹדֶה, וְכָל לָשׁוֹן לְךָ תִּשָּׁבַע, וְכָל בֶּרֶךְ לְךָ תִכְרַע, וְכָל קוֹמָה לְפָנֶיךָ תִשְׁתַּחֲוֶה, וְכָל לְבָבוֹת יִירָאוּךָ, וְכָל קֶרֶב וּכְלָיוֹת יְזַמְּרוּ לִשְׁמֶךָ. כַּדָּבָר שֶׁכָּתוּב (תהלים לה, י), "כָּל עַצְמוֹתַי תֹּאמַרְנָה, ה' מִי כָמוֹךָ מַצִּיל עָנִי מֵחָזָק מִמֶּנּוּ וְעָנִי וְאֶבְיוֹן מִגֹּזְלוֹ." מִי יִדְמֶה לָּךְ וּמִי יִשְׁוֶה לָּךְ וּמִי יַעֲרָךְ לָךְ הָאֵל הַגָּדוֹל, הַגִּבּוֹר וְהַנּוֹרָא, אֵל עֶלְיוֹן, קֹנֵה שָׁמַיִם וָאָרֶץ. נְהַלֶּלְךָ וּנְשַׁבֵּחֲךָ וּנְפָאֶרְךָ וּנְבָרֵךְ אֶת שֵׁם קָדְשֶׁךָ, כָּאָמוּר (תהלים קג, א): "לְדָוִד, בָּרְכִי נַפְשִׁי אֶת ה' וְכָל קְרָבַי אֶת שֵׁם קָדְשׁוֹ."

הָאֵל בְּתַעֲצֻמוֹת עֻזֶּךָ, הַגָּדוֹל בִּכְבוֹד שְׁמֶךָ, הַגִּבּוֹר לָנֶצַח וְהַנּוֹרָא בְּנוֹרְאוֹתֶיךָ, הַמֶּלֶךְ הַיּוֹשֵׁב עַל כִּסֵּא רָם וְנִשָּׂא.

שׁוֹכֵן עַד מָרוֹם וְקָדוֹשׁ שְׁמוֹ. וְכָתוּב (תהלים לג, א): "רַנְּנוּ צַדִּיקִים בַּה', לַיְשָׁרִים נָאוָה תְהִלָּה." בְּפִי

the upright You shall be praised; By the lips of the righteous shall You be blessed; By the tongue of the devout shall You be exalted; And among the holy shall You be sanctified.

And in the assemblies of the myriads of Your people, the House of Israel, in joyous song will Your name be glorified, our King, in each and every generation; as it is the duty of all creatures, before You, Lord our God, and God of our ancestors, to thank, to praise, to extol, to glorify, to exalt, to lavish, to bless, to raise high and to acclaim - beyond the words of the songs and praises of David, the son of Yishai, Your servant, Your anointed one.

May Your name be praised forever, our King, the Power, the Great and holy King - in the heavens and in the earth. Since for You it is pleasant - O Lord our God and God of our ancestors - song and lauding, praise and hymn, boldness and dominion, triumph, greatness and strength, psalm and splendor, holiness and kingship, blessings and thanksgivings, from now and forever. Blessed are You Lord, Power, King exalted through laudings, Power of thanksgivings, Master of Wonders, who chooses the songs of hymn - King, Power of the life of the worlds.

FOURTH CUP OF WINE

Raise the cup and say:

Blessed are You, Lord our God, King of the universe, who creates the fruit of the vine.

We drink while reclining to the left.

יְשָׁרִים תִּתְהַלָּל, וּבְדִבְרֵי צַדִּיקִים תִּתְבָּרַךְ, וּבִלְשׁוֹן חֲסִידִים תִּתְרוֹמָם, וּבְקֶרֶב קְדוֹשִׁים תִּתְקַדָּשׁ.

וּבְמַקְהֲלוֹת רִבְבוֹת עַמְּךָ בֵּית יִשְׂרָאֵל בְּרִנָּה יִתְפָּאֵר שִׁמְךָ, מַלְכֵּנוּ, בְּכָל דּוֹר וָדוֹר, שֶׁכֵּן חוֹבַת כָּל הַיְצוּרִים לְפָנֶיךָ, ה' אֱלֹהֵינוּ וֵאלֹהֵי אֲבוֹתֵינוּ, לְהוֹדוֹת לְהַלֵּל לְשַׁבֵּחַ, לְפָאֵר לְרוֹמֵם לְהַדֵּר לְבָרֵךְ, לְעַלֵּה וּלְקַלֵּס עַל כָּל דִּבְרֵי שִׁירוֹת וְתִשְׁבְּחוֹת דָּוִד בֶּן יִשַׁי עַבְדְּךָ מְשִׁיחֶךָ.

יִשְׁתַּבַּח שִׁמְךָ לָעַד מַלְכֵּנוּ, הָאֵל הַמֶּלֶךְ הַגָּדוֹל וְהַקָּדוֹשׁ בַּשָּׁמַיִם וּבָאָרֶץ, כִּי לְךָ נָאֶה, ה' אֱלֹהֵינוּ וֵאלֹהֵי אֲבוֹתֵינוּ, שִׁיר וּשְׁבָחָה, הַלֵּל וְזִמְרָה, עֹז וּמֶמְשָׁלָה, נֶצַח, גְּדֻלָּה וּגְבוּרָה, תְּהִלָּה וְתִפְאֶרֶת, קְדֻשָּׁה וּמַלְכוּת, בְּרָכוֹת וְהוֹדָאוֹת מֵעַתָּה וְעַד עוֹלָם. בָּרוּךְ אַתָּה ה', אֵל מֶלֶךְ גָּדוֹל בַּתִּשְׁבָּחוֹת, אֵל הַהוֹדָאוֹת, אֲדוֹן הַנִּפְלָאוֹת, הַבּוֹחֵר בְּשִׁירֵי זִמְרָה, מֶלֶךְ אֵל חֵי הָעוֹלָמִים.

כוס רביעית

Raise the cup and say:

בָּרוּךְ אַתָּה ה', אֱלֹהֵינוּ מֶלֶךְ הָעוֹלָם, בּוֹרֵא פְּרִי הַגָּפֶן.

We drink while reclining to the left.

Blessed are You, Lord our God, King of the universe, for the vine and for the fruit of the vine; and for the bounty of the field; and for a desirable, good and broad land, which You wanted to give to our fathers, to eat from its fruit and to be satiated from its goodness. Please have mercy, Lord our God upon Israel Your people; and upon Jerusalem, Your city: and upon Zion, the dwelling place of Your glory; and upon Your altar; and upon Your sanctuary; and build Jerusalem Your holy city quickly in our days, and bring us up into it and gladden us in its building; and we shall eat from its fruit, and be satiated from its goodness, and bless You in holiness and purity. [On Shabbat: And may you be pleased to embolden us on this Shabbat day] and gladden us on this day of the Festival of Matzot. Since You, Lord, are good and do good to all, we thank You for the land and for the fruit of *the vine. Blessed are You, Lord, for the land and for the fruit of *the vine. [*if the wine is from Israel: her vine]

Accepted

Completed is the Seder of Passover according to its law, according to all its judgement and statute. Just as we have merited to arrange it, so too, may we merit to do its sacrifice. Pure One who dwells in the habitation, raise up the countless congregation of the community. Bring close, lead the plantings of the sapling, redeemed, to Zion in joy.

THE (UNOFFICIAL) SEINFELD HAGGADAH

בָּרוּךְ אַתָּה ה' אֱלֹהֵינוּ מֶלֶךְ הָעוֹלָם, עַל הַגֶּפֶן וְעַל פְּרִי הַגֶּפֶן, עַל תְּנוּבַת הַשָּׂדֶה וְעַל אֶרֶץ חֶמְדָּה טוֹבָה וּרְחָבָה שֶׁרָצִיתָ וְהִנְחַלְתָּ לַאֲבוֹתֵינוּ לֶאֱכוֹל מִפִּרְיָהּ וְלִשְׂבּוֹעַ מִטּוּבָהּ. רַחֶם נָא ה' אֱלֹהֵינוּ עַל יִשְׂרָאֵל עַמֶּךָ וְעַל יְרוּשָׁלַיִם עִירֶךָ וְעַל צִיּוֹן מִשְׁכַּן כְּבוֹדֶךָ וְעַל מִזְבְּחֶךָ וְעַל הֵיכָלֶךָ וּבְנֵה יְרוּשָׁלַיִם עִיר הַקֹּדֶשׁ בִּמְהֵרָה בְיָמֵינוּ וְהַעֲלֵנוּ לְתוֹכָהּ וְשַׂמְּחֵנוּ בְּבִנְיָנָהּ וְנֹאכַל מִפִּרְיָהּ וְנִשְׂבַּע מִטּוּבָהּ וּנְבָרֶכְךָ עָלֶיהָ בִּקְדֻשָּׁה וּבְטָהֳרָה [בשבת: וּרְצֵה וְהַחֲלִיצֵנוּ בְּיוֹם הַשַּׁבָּת הַזֶּה] וְשַׂמְּחֵנוּ בְּיוֹם חַג הַמַּצּוֹת הַזֶּה, כִּי אַתָּה ה' טוֹב וּמֵטִיב לַכֹּל, וְנוֹדֶה לְךָ עַל הָאָרֶץ וְעַל פְּרִי הַגֶּפֶן. בָּרוּךְ אַתָּה ה', עַל הָאָרֶץ וְעַל פְּרִי הַגֶּפֶן.* [*אם היין מארץ ישראל: גַּפְנָהּ]

נרצה

חֲסַל סִדּוּר פֶּסַח כְּהִלְכָתוֹ, כְּכָל מִשְׁפָּטוֹ וְחֻקָּתוֹ. כַּאֲשֶׁר זָכִינוּ לְסַדֵּר אוֹתוֹ כֵּן נִזְכֶּה לַעֲשׂוֹתוֹ. זָךְ שׁוֹכֵן מְעוֹנָה, קוֹמֵם קְהַל עֲדַת מִי מָנָה. בְּקָרוֹב נַהֵל נִטְעֵי כַנָּה פְּדוּיִים לְצִיּוֹן בְּרִנָּה.

THE HAGGADAH ABOUT NOTHING

Next year, let us be in the built Jerusalem! Because, believe it or not, we aren't at home, please leave a message at the beep, we must be out or we'd pick up the phone, where could we be? Believe it or not we're not home[81]!

On the first night we say:

And so, it was in the middle of the night.
Then, most of the miracles did You wondrously do at night, at the first of the watches this night.
A righteous convert did you make victorious when it was divided for him at night [referring to Avraham in his war against the four kings - Genesis 14:15], and it was in the middle of the night.
You judged the king of Gerar [Avimelekh] in a dream of the night; you frightened an Aramean [Lavan] in the dark of the night;
and Yisrael dominated an angel and was able to withstand him at night [Genesis 32:25-30], and it was in the middle of the night.
You crushed the firstborn of Patros [Pharaoh, as per Ezekiel 30:14] in the middle of the night, their wealth they did not find when they got up at night; the attack of the leader Charoshet [Sisera] did you sweep away by the stars of the night [Judges 5:20], and it was in the middle of the night.
The blasphemer [Sancheriv whose servants blasphemed when trying to discourage the inhabitants of Jerusalem] counseled to wave off the desired ones, You made him wear his corpses on his head at night [II Kings 19:35]; Bel and his pedestal were bent in the pitch of night [in Nevuchadnezar's dream in Daniel 2]; to the man of delight [Daniel] was revealed the

THE (UNOFFICIAL) SEINFELD HAGGADAH

לְשָׁנָה הַבָּאָה בִּירוּשָׁלַיִם הַבְּנוּיָה.

On the first night we say:

וּבְכֵן, וַיְהִי בַּחֲצִי הַלַּיְלָה.
אָז רוֹב נִסִּים הִפְלֵאתָ בַּלַּיְלָה,
בְּרֹאשׁ אַשְׁמוֹרֶת זֶה הַלַּיְלָה.
גֵּר צֶדֶק נִצַּחְתּוֹ כְּנֶחֱלַק לוֹ לַיְלָה,
וַיְהִי בַּחֲצִי הַלַּיְלָה.

דַּנְתָּ מֶלֶךְ גְּרָר בַּחֲלוֹם הַלַּיְלָה,
הִפְחַדְתָּ אֲרַמִּי בְּאֶמֶשׁ לַיְלָה,
וַיָּשַׂר יִשְׂרָאֵל לְמַלְאָךְ וַיּוּכַל לוֹ לַיְלָה,
וַיְהִי בַּחֲצִי הַלַּיְלָה.

זֶרַע בְּכוֹרֵי פַתְרוֹס מָחַצְתָּ בַּחֲצִי הַלַּיְלָה,
חֵילָם לֹא מָצְאוּ בְּקוּמָם בַּלַּיְלָה,
טִיסַת נְגִיד חֲרֹשֶׁת סִלִּיתָ בְּכוֹכְבֵי לַיְלָה,
וַיְהִי בַּחֲצִי הַלַּיְלָה.

יָעַץ מְחָרֵף לְנוֹפֵף אִוּוּי, הוֹבַשְׁתָּ פְגָרָיו בַּלַּיְלָה,
כָּרַע בֵּל וּמַצָּבוֹ בְּאִישׁוֹן לַיְלָה,
לְאִישׁ חֲמוּדוֹת נִגְלָה רָז חֲזוֹת לַיְלָה,
וַיְהִי בַּחֲצִי הַלַּיְלָה.

נרצה — 143

secret visions at night, and it was in the middle of the night. The one who got drunk [Balshatsar] from the holy vessels was killed on that night [Daniel 5:30], the one saved from the pit of lions [Daniel] interpreted the scary visions of the night; hatred was preserved by the Agagite [Haman] and he wrote books at night, and it was in the middle of the night.

You aroused your victory upon him by disturbing the sleep of night [of Achashverosh], You will stomp the wine press for the one who guards from anything at night [Esav/Seir as per Isaiah 21:11]; He yelled like a guard and spoke, "the morning has come and also the night," and it was in the middle of the night.

Bring close the day which is not day and not night [referring to the end of days - Zechariah 14:7], High One, make known that Yours is the day and also Yours is the night, guards appoint for Your city all the day and all the night, illuminate like the light of the day, the darkness of the night, as bright as a Kenny Rogers Roaster sign[82] and it was in the middle of the night.

On the second night outside of Israel we say:

And so "And you shall say, 'it is the Passover sacrifice'" (Exodus 12:42).
The boldness of Your strong deeds did you wondrously show at Passover; at the head of all the holidays did You raise Passover; You revealed to the Ezrachite [Avraham], midnight of the night of Passover. "And you shall say, 'it is the Passover sacrifice.'"
Upon his doors did You knock at the heat of the day on Passover [Genesis 18:1]; he sustained shining ones [angels]

THE (UNOFFICIAL) SEINFELD HAGGADAH

מִשְׁתַּכֵּר בִּכְלֵי קֹדֶשׁ נֶהֱרַג בּוֹ בַּלַּיְלָה,
נוֹשַׁע מִבּוֹר אֲרָיוֹת פּוֹתֵר בִּעֲתוּתֵי לַיְלָה,
שִׂנְאָה נָטַר אֲגָגִי וְכָתַב סְפָרִים בַּלַּיְלָה,
וַיְהִי בַּחֲצִי הַלַּיְלָה.

עוֹרַרְתָּ נִצְחֲךָ עָלָיו בְּנֶדֶד שְׁנַת לַיְלָה.
פּוּרָה תִדְרוֹךְ לְשׁוֹמֵר מַה מִּלַּיְלָה,
צָרַח כַּשּׁוֹמֵר וְשָׂח אָתָא בֹקֶר וְגַם לַיְלָה,
וַיְהִי בַּחֲצִי הַלַּיְלָה.

קָרֵב יוֹם אֲשֶׁר הוּא לֹא יוֹם וְלֹא לַיְלָה,
רָם הוֹדַע כִּי לְךָ הַיּוֹם אַף לְךָ הַלַּיְלָה,
שׁוֹמְרִים הַפְקֵד לְעִירְךָ כָּל הַיּוֹם וְכָל הַלַּיְלָה,
תָּאִיר כְּאוֹר יוֹם חֶשְׁכַּת לַיְלָה,
וַיְהִי בַּחֲצִי הַלַּיְלָה.

On the second night outside of Israel we say:

וּבְכֵן "וַאֲמַרְתֶּם 'זֶבַח פֶּסַח'" (שמות יב, מב).
אֹמֶץ גְּבוּרוֹתֶיךָ הִפְלֵאתָ בַּפֶּסַח,
בְּרֹאשׁ כָּל מוֹעֲדוֹת נִשֵּׂאתָ פֶּסַח.
גִּלִּיתָ לְאֶזְרָחִי חֲצוֹת לֵיל פֶּסַח,
"וַאֲמַרְתֶּם 'זֶבַח פֶּסַח'."

דְּלָתָיו דָּפַקְתָּ כְּחֹם הַיּוֹם בַּפֶּסַח,
הִסְעִיד נוֹצְצִים עֻגוֹת מַצּוֹת בַּפֶּסַח,

145 — נרצה

with cakes of matzah on Passover; and to the cattle he ran, in commemoration of the bull that was set up for Passover. "And you shall say, 'it is the Passover sacrifice.'"

The Sodomites caused Him indignation and He set them on fire on Passover; Lot was rescued from them and matzot did he bake at the end of Passover; He swept the land of Mof and Nof [cities in Egypt] on Passover. "And you shall say, 'it is the Passover sacrifice.'"

The head of every firstborn did You crush on the guarded night of Passover; Powerful One, over the firstborn son did You pass over with the blood on Passover; so as to not let the destroyer come into my gates on Passover. "And you shall say, 'it is the Passover sacrifice.'"

The enclosed one [Jericho] was enclosed in the season of Passover; Midian was destroyed with a portion of the omer-barley on Passover [via Gideon, as per Judges 7]; from the fat of Pul and Lud [Assyrian soldiers of Sancheriv] was burnt in pyres on Passover. "And you shall say, 'it is the Passover sacrifice.'"

Still today [Sancheriv will go no further than] to stand in Nov [Isaiah 10:32], until he cried at the time of Passover; a palm of the hand wrote [Daniel 5:5] to rip up the deep one [the Bayblonian one - Balshatsar] on Passover; set up the watch, set the table [referring to Balshatsar, based on Psalms 21:5] on Passover. "And you shall say, 'it is the Passover sacrifice.'"

The congregation did Hadassah [Esther] bring in to triple a fast on Passover; the head of the house of evil [Haman] did you crush on a tree of fifty [amot] on Passover; these two [plagues as per Isaiah 47:9] will you bring in an instant to the Utsi [Esav] on Passover; embolden Your hand, raise Your

וְאֶל הַבָּקָר רָץ זֵכֶר לְשׁוֹר עֵרֶךְ פֶּסַח,
"וַאֲמַרְתֶּם 'זֶבַח פֶּסַח.'"

זוֹעֲמוּ סְדוֹמִים וְלוֹהֲטוּ בָּאֵשׁ בַּפֶּסַח,
חֻלַּץ לוֹט מֵהֶם וּמַצּוֹת אָפָה בְקֵץ פֶּסַח,
טִאטֵאתָ אַדְמַת מוֹף וְנוֹף בְּעָבְרְךָ בַּפֶּסַח.
"וַאֲמַרְתֶּם 'זֶבַח פֶּסַח.'"

יָהּ רֹאשׁ כָּל הוֹן מָחַצְתָּ בְּלֵיל שִׁמּוּר פֶּסַח,
כַּבִּיר, עַל בֵּן בְּכוֹר פָּסַחְתָּ בְּדַם פֶּסַח,
לְבִלְתִּי תֵּת מַשְׁחִית לָבֹא בִּפְתָחַי בַּפֶּסַח,
"וַאֲמַרְתֶּם 'זֶבַח פֶּסַח.'"

מְסֻגֶּרֶת סֻגְּרָה בְּעִתּוֹתֵי פֶּסַח,
נִשְׁמְדָה מִדְיָן בִּצְלִיל שְׂעוֹרֵי עֹמֶר פֶּסַח,
שׂוֹרְפוּ מִשְׁמַנֵּי פּוּל וְלוּד בִּיקַד יְקוֹד פֶּסַח,
"וַאֲמַרְתֶּם 'זֶבַח פֶּסַח.'"

עוֹד הַיּוֹם בְּנֹב לַעֲמוֹד עַד גָּעָה עוֹנַת פֶּסַח,
פַּס יַד כָּתְבָה לְקַעֲקֵעַ צוּל בַּפֶּסַח,
צָפֹה הַצָּפִית עֲרוֹךְ הַשֻּׁלְחָן בַּפֶּסַח.
"וַאֲמַרְתֶּם 'זֶבַח פֶּסַח.'"

קָהָל כִּנְּסָה הֲדַסָּה לְשַׁלֵּשׁ צוֹם בַּפֶּסַח,
רֹאשׁ מִבֵּית רָשָׁע מָחַצְתָּ בְּעֵץ חֲמִשִּׁים בַּפֶּסַח,
שְׁתֵּי אֵלֶּה רֶגַע תָּבִיא לְעוּצִית בַּפֶּסַח,

147 — נרצה

right hand, as on the night You were sanctified on the festival of Passover. "And you shall say, 'it is the Passover sacrifice.'"

COUNTING THE OMER

We count the first night of the Omer on the second night of Passover:

Blessed are You, Lord our God, King of the Universe, who has sanctified us with His commandments and has commanded us on the counting of the omer. Today is day one of the Omer.

KI LO NA'EH

On both nights, continue here.

Since for Him it is pleasant, like the purest syrup nectar Bosco[83], for Him it is suited.
Mighty in rulership, properly chosen, his troops shall say to Him, "Yours and Yours, Yours since it is Yours, Yours and even Yours, Yours, Lord is the kingdom; since for Him it is pleasant, for Him it is suited."

BEE BA DO DUM DUM, BUM BADUM BUM BUH, BAH DUH, BAH DAH DUM DUM, DUM DEDUM DUM DUM DUM DUM. BADA DO DUM DEDUM.

The Counting

Starting on the second day of Pesach, we begin to count until the holiday of Shavuot, called Sefirat Haomer. Every night for 49 nights we count up until we reach the culmination of the period of Exodus, when God gives His Torah to His newly redeemed nation. The obligation is to count each night with blessing. If you forget one night, you can still count the next night, but only if you counted the missed night during the day. Rabbi Soleveitchik explains that when you miss a night, counting during the day does not make it up. However, for the next night, you can only count the next number if the number before it was counted. For example, if you missed day six completely, you cannot count day seven because counting definitionally happens sequentially. Therefore, we put the first night in the Haggadah because it's always embarrassing to forget right away.

THE (UNOFFICIAL) SEINFELD HAGGADAH

תָּעֹז יָדְךָ תָּרוּם יְמִינְךָ כְּלֵיל הִתְקַדֵּשׁ חַג פֶּסַח, "וַאֲמַרְתֶּם 'זֶבַח פֶּסַח.'"

ספירת העומר

We count the first night of the Omer on the second night of Passover:

בָּרוּךְ אַתָּה ה', אֱלֹהֵינוּ מֶלֶךְ הָעוֹלָם, אֲשֶׁר קִדְּשָׁנוּ בְּמִצְוֹתָיו וְצִוָּנוּ עַל סְפִירַת הָעוֹמֶר. הַיּוֹם יוֹם אֶחָד בָּעוֹמֶר.

כי לו נאה

On both nights, continue here.

כִּי לוֹ נָאֶה, כִּי לוֹ יָאֶה.
אַדִּיר בִּמְלוּכָה, בָּחוּר כַּהֲלָכָה, גְּדוּדָיו יֹאמְרוּ לוֹ: לְךָ וּלְךָ, לְךָ כִּי לְךָ, לְךָ אַף לְךָ, לְךָ ה' הַמַּמְלָכָה, כִּי לוֹ נָאֶה, כִּי לוֹ יָאֶה.

בִּי בַּה דוּ דוּם דוּם, בּוֹם בְּדוּם בּוֹם בּוֹ, בַּה דוּ, בַּה דַה דוּם דוּם, דוּם דְדוּם דוּם דוּם דוּם. בַּדַה דוּ דוּם דוּם.

The counting of the Omer is not unlike the male relationships in *Seinfeld*. In "The Boyfriend[C151]," Jerry meets his idol, Keith Hernandez, the legendary New York Mets first baseman, and they become friends. After hanging out one night, Keith calls Jerry to ask him to help him move to a new apartment. Jerry is so taken aback that he says yes, but "hardly feels right about it, I hardly know the guy. That's a big step in a male relationship, like going all the way." Kramer is absolutely shocked, "what a nerve...you're not going to do it are you? Don't you have any pride or self respect? What are you going to do, start driving him to the airport?" What both Jerry and Kramer understand is that relationships, and especially friendships, have to be built step by step. They sure would have been able to count the Omer correctly, but I have little faith that Keith Hernandez would.

נרצה — 149

Noted in rulership, properly splendid, His distinguished ones will say to him, "Yours and Yours, Yours since it is Yours, Yours and even Yours, Yours, Lord is the kingdom; since for Him it is pleasant, for Him it is suited."

Meritorious in rulership, properly robust, His scribes shall say to him, "Yours and Yours, Yours since it is Yours, Yours and even Yours, Yours, Lord is the kingdom; since for Him it is pleasant, for Him it is suited."

Unique in rulership, properly powerful, His wise ones say to Him, "Yours and Yours, Yours since it is Yours, Yours and even Yours, Yours, Lord is the kingdom; since for Him it is pleasant, for Him it is suited."

Reigning in rulership, properly awesome, those around Him say to Him, "Yours and Yours, Yours since it is Yours, Yours and even Yours, Yours, Lord is the kingdom; since for Him it is pleasant, for Him it is suited."

Humble in rulership, properly restoring, His righteous ones say to Him, "Yours and Yours, Yours since it is Yours, Yours and even Yours, Yours, Lord is the kingdom; since for Him it is pleasant, for Him it is suited."

Holy in rulership, properly merciful, His angels say to Him, "Yours and Yours, Yours since it is Yours, Yours and even Yours, Yours, Lord is the kingdom; since for Him it is pleasant, for Him it is suited."

Dynamic in rulership, properly supportive, His innocent ones say to Him, "Yours and Yours, Yours since it is Yours, Yours and even Yours, Yours, Lord is the kingdom; since for Him it is pleasant, for Him it is suited."

THE (UNOFFICIAL) SEINFELD HAGGADAH

דָּגוּל בִּמְלוּכָה, הָדוּר כַּהֲלָכָה, וָתִיקָיו יֹאמְרוּ לוֹ: לְךָ וּלְךָ, לְךָ כִּי לְךָ, לְךָ אַף לְךָ, לְךָ ה' הַמַּמְלָכָה, כִּי לוֹ נָאֶה, כִּי לוֹ יָאֶה.

זַכַּאי בִּמְלוּכָה, חָסִין כַּהֲלָכָה טַפְסְרָיו יֹאמְרוּ לוֹ: לְךָ וּלְךָ, לְךָ כִּי לְךָ, לְךָ אַף לְךָ, לְךָ ה' הַמַּמְלָכָה, כִּי לוֹ נָאֶה, כִּי לוֹ יָאֶה.

יָחִיד בִּמְלוּכָה, כַּבִּיר כַּהֲלָכָה לִמּוּדָיו יֹאמְרוּ לוֹ: לְךָ וּלְךָ, לְךָ כִּי לְךָ, לְךָ אַף לְךָ, לְךָ ה' הַמַּמְלָכָה, כִּי לוֹ נָאֶה, כִּי לוֹ יָאֶה.

מוֹשֵׁל בִּמְלוּכָה, נוֹרָא כַּהֲלָכָה סְבִיבָיו יֹאמְרוּ לוֹ: לְךָ וּלְךָ, לְךָ כִּי לְךָ, לְךָ אַף לְךָ, לְךָ ה' הַמַּמְלָכָה, כִּי לוֹ נָאֶה, כִּי לוֹ יָאֶה.

עָנָיו בִּמְלוּכָה, פּוֹדֶה כַּהֲלָכָה, צַדִּיקָיו יֹאמְרוּ לוֹ: לְךָ וּלְךָ, לְךָ כִּי לְךָ, לְךָ אַף לְךָ, לְךָ ה' הַמַּמְלָכָה, כִּי לוֹ נָאֶה, כִּי לוֹ יָאֶה.

קָדוֹשׁ בִּמְלוּכָה, רַחוּם כַּהֲלָכָה שִׁנְאַנָּיו יֹאמְרוּ לוֹ: לְךָ וּלְךָ, לְךָ כִּי לְךָ, לְךָ אַף לְךָ, לְךָ ה' הַמַּמְלָכָה, כִּי לוֹ נָאֶה, כִּי לוֹ יָאֶה.

תַּקִּיף בִּמְלוּכָה, תּוֹמֵךְ כַּהֲלָכָה תְּמִימָיו יֹאמְרוּ לוֹ: לְךָ וּלְךָ, לְךָ כִּי לְךָ, לְךָ אַף לְךָ, לְךָ ה' הַמַּמְלָכָה, כִּי לוֹ נָאֶה, כִּי לוֹ יָאֶה.

ADIR HU

Mighty is He, may He build His house soon. Quickly, quickly, in our days, soon. God build, God build, build Your house soon.

Chosen is He, great is He, noted is He. Quickly, quickly, in our days, soon. God build, God build, build Your house soon.

Splendid is He, distinguished is He, meritorious is He. Quickly, quickly, in our days, soon. God build, God build, build Your house soon.

Pious is He, pure is He, unique is He. Quickly, quickly, in our days, soon. God build, God build, build Your house soon.

Powerful is He, wise is He, A king is He. Quickly, quickly, in our days, soon. God build, God build, build Your house soon.

Awesome is He, exalted is He, heroic is He. Quickly, quickly, in our days, soon. God build, God build, build Your house soon.

A restorer is He, righteous is He, holy is He. Quickly, quickly, in our days, soon. God build, God build, build Your house soon.

Merciful is He, the Omnipotent is He, dynamic is He. Quickly, quickly, in our days, soon. God build, God build, build Your house soon.

אדיר הוא

אַדִּיר הוּא יִבְנֶה בֵּיתוֹ בְּקָרוֹב. בִּמְהֵרָה, בִּמְהֵרָה, בְּיָמֵינוּ בְּקָרוֹב. אֵל בְּנֵה, אֵל בְּנֵה, בְּנֵה בֵיתְךָ בְּקָרוֹב.

בָּחוּר הוּא, גָּדוֹל הוּא, דָּגוּל הוּא יִבְנֶה בֵּיתוֹ בְּקָרוֹב. בִּמְהֵרָה, בִּמְהֵרָה, בְּיָמֵינוּ בְּקָרוֹב. אֵל בְּנֵה, אֵל בְּנֵה, בְּנֵה בֵיתְךָ בְּקָרוֹב.

הָדוּר הוּא, וָתִיק הוּא, זַכַּאי הוּא יִבְנֶה בֵּיתוֹ בְּקָרוֹב. בִּמְהֵרָה, בִּמְהֵרָה, בְּיָמֵינוּ בְּקָרוֹב. אֵל בְּנֵה, אֵל בְּנֵה, בְּנֵה בֵיתְךָ בְּקָרוֹב.

חָסִיד הוּא, טָהוֹר הוּא, יָחִיד הוּא יִבְנֶה בֵּיתוֹ בְּקָרוֹב. בִּמְהֵרָה, בִּמְהֵרָה, בְּיָמֵינוּ בְּקָרוֹב. אֵל בְּנֵה, אֵל בְּנֵה, בְּנֵה בֵיתְךָ בְּקָרוֹב.

כַּבִּיר הוּא, לָמוּד הוּא, מֶלֶךְ הוּא יִבְנֶה בֵּיתוֹ בְּקָרוֹב. בִּמְהֵרָה, בִּמְהֵרָה, בְּיָמֵינוּ בְּקָרוֹב. אֵל בְּנֵה, אֵל בְּנֵה, בְּנֵה בֵיתְךָ בְּקָרוֹב.

נוֹרָא הוּא, סַגִּיב הוּא, עִזּוּז הוּא יִבְנֶה בֵּיתוֹ בְּקָרוֹב. בִּמְהֵרָה, בִּמְהֵרָה, בְּיָמֵינוּ בְּקָרוֹב. אֵל בְּנֵה, אֵל בְּנֵה, בְּנֵה בֵיתְךָ בְּקָרוֹב.

פּוֹדֶה הוּא, צַדִּיק הוּא, קָדוֹשׁ הוּא יִבְנֶה בֵּיתוֹ בְּקָרוֹב. בִּמְהֵרָה, בִּמְהֵרָה, בְּיָמֵינוּ בְּקָרוֹב. אֵל בְּנֵה, אֵל בְּנֵה, בְּנֵה בֵיתְךָ בְּקָרוֹב.

רַחוּם הוּא, שַׁדַּי הוּא, תַּקִּיף הוּא יִבְנֶה בֵּיתוֹ בְּקָרוֹב. בִּמְהֵרָה, בִּמְהֵרָה, בְּיָמֵינוּ בְּקָרוֹב. אֵל בְּנֵה, אֵל בְּנֵה, בְּנֵה בֵיתְךָ בְּקָרוֹב.

WHO KNOWS ONE?

Who knows **one**? I know one: One is our God in the heavens and the earth.

Who knows **two**? I know two: two are the tablets of the covenant, One is our God in the heavens and the earth.

Who knows **three**? I know three: three are the fathers, two are the tablets of the covenant, One is our God in the heavens and the earth.

Who knows **four**? I know four: four are the mothers, three are the fathers, two are the tablets of the covenant, One is our God in the heavens and the earth.

Who knows **five**? I know five: five are the books of the Torah, four are the mothers, three are the fathers, two are the tablets of the covenant, One is our God in the heavens and the earth.

Who knows **six**? I know six: six are the orders of the Mishnah, five are the books of the Torah, four are the mothers, three are the fathers, two are the tablets of the covenant, One is our God in the heavens and the earth.

Who knows **seven**? I know seven: seven are the days of the week and also the name of George's imaginary child[84], six are the orders of the Mishnah, five are the books of the Torah, four are the mothers, three are the fathers, two are the tablets of the covenant, One is our God in the heavens and the earth.

Who knows **eight**? I know eight: eight are the days of circumcision, seven are the days of the week, six are the orders of the Mishnah, five are the books of the Torah, four are the mothers, three are the fathers, two are the tablets of the covenant, One is our God in the heavens and the earth.

Who knows **nine**? I know nine: nine are the months of birth,

אחד מי יודע

אֶחָד מִי יוֹדֵעַ? אֶחָד אֲנִי יוֹדֵעַ: אֶחָד אֱלֹהֵינוּ שֶׁבַּשָּׁמַיִם וּבָאָרֶץ.

שְׁנַיִם מִי יוֹדֵעַ? שְׁנַיִם אֲנִי יוֹדֵעַ: שְׁנֵי לֻחוֹת הַבְּרִית. אֶחָד אֱלֹהֵינוּ שֶׁבַּשָּׁמַיִם וּבָאָרֶץ.

שְׁלֹשָׁה מִי יוֹדֵעַ? שְׁלֹשָׁה אֲנִי יוֹדֵעַ: שְׁלֹשָׁה אָבוֹת, שְׁנֵי לֻחוֹת הַבְּרִית, אֶחָד אֱלֹהֵינוּ שֶׁבַּשָּׁמַיִם וּבָאָרֶץ.

אַרְבַּע מִי יוֹדֵעַ? אַרְבַּע אֲנִי יוֹדֵעַ: אַרְבַּע אִמָּהוֹת, שְׁלֹשָׁה אָבוֹת, שְׁנֵי לֻחוֹת הַבְּרִית, אֶחָד אֱלֹהֵינוּ שֶׁבַּשָּׁמַיִם וּבָאָרֶץ.

חֲמִשָּׁה מִי יוֹדֵעַ? חֲמִשָּׁה אֲנִי יוֹדֵעַ: חֲמִשָּׁה חוּמְשֵׁי תוֹרָה, אַרְבַּע אִמָּהוֹת, שְׁלֹשָׁה אָבוֹת, שְׁנֵי לֻחוֹת הַבְּרִית, אֶחָד אֱלֹהֵינוּ שֶׁבַּשָּׁמַיִם וּבָאָרֶץ.

שִׁשָּׁה מִי יוֹדֵעַ? שִׁשָּׁה אֲנִי יוֹדֵעַ: שִׁשָּׁה סִדְרֵי מִשְׁנָה, חֲמִשָּׁה חוּמְשֵׁי תוֹרָה, אַרְבַּע אִמָּהוֹת, שְׁלֹשָׁה אָבוֹת, שְׁנֵי לֻחוֹת הַבְּרִית, אֶחָד אֱלֹהֵינוּ שֶׁבַּשָּׁמַיִם וּבָאָרֶץ.

שִׁבְעָה מִי יוֹדֵעַ? שִׁבְעָה אֲנִי יוֹדֵעַ: שִׁבְעָה יְמֵי שַׁבָּתָא, שִׁשָּׁה סִדְרֵי מִשְׁנָה, חֲמִשָּׁה חוּמְשֵׁי תוֹרָה, אַרְבַּע אִמָּהוֹת, שְׁלֹשָׁה אָבוֹת, שְׁנֵי לֻחוֹת הַבְּרִית, אֶחָד אֱלֹהֵינוּ שֶׁבַּשָּׁמַיִם וּבָאָרֶץ.

שְׁמוֹנָה מִי יוֹדֵעַ? שְׁמוֹנָה אֲנִי יוֹדֵעַ: שְׁמוֹנָה יְמֵי מִילָה, שִׁבְעָה יְמֵי שַׁבָּתָא, שִׁשָּׁה סִדְרֵי מִשְׁנָה, חֲמִשָּׁה חוּמְשֵׁי תוֹרָה, אַרְבַּע אִמָּהוֹת, שְׁלֹשָׁה אָבוֹת, שְׁנֵי לֻחוֹת הַבְּרִית, אֶחָד אֱלֹהֵינוּ שֶׁבַּשָּׁמַיִם וּבָאָרֶץ.

eight are the days of circumcision, seven are the days of the week, six are the orders of the Mishnah, five are the books of the Torah, four are the mothers, three are the fathers, two are the tablets of the covenant, One is our God in the heavens and the earth.

Who knows **ten**? I know ten: ten are the statements, nine are the months of birth, eight are the days of circumcision, seven are the days of the week, six are the orders of the Mishnah, five are the books of the Torah, four are the mothers, three are the fathers, two are the tablets of the covenant, One is our God in the heavens and the earth.

Who knows **eleven**? I know eleven: eleven are the stars of Yosef's dream, ten are the statements, nine are the months of birth, eight are the days of circumcision, seven are the days of the week, six are the orders of the Mishnah, five are the books of the Torah, four are the mothers, three are the fathers, two are the tablets of the covenant, One is our God in the heavens and the earth.

Who knows **twelve**? I know twelve: twelve are the tribes, eleven are the stars, ten are the statements, nine are the months of birth, eight are the days of circumcision, seven are the days of the week, six are the orders of the Mishnah, five are the books of the Torah, four are the mothers, three are the fathers, two are the tablets of the covenant, One is our God in the heavens and the earth.

Who knows **thirteen**? I know thirteen: thirteen are the characteristics, twelve are the tribes, eleven are the stars, ten are the statements, nine are the months of birth, eight are the days of circumcision, seven are the days of the week, six are the orders of the Mishnah, five are the books of the Torah,

THE (UNOFFICIAL) SEINFELD HAGGADAH

תִּשְׁעָה מִי יוֹדֵעַ? תִּשְׁעָה אֲנִי יוֹדֵעַ: תִּשְׁעָה יַרְחֵי לֵדָה, שְׁמוֹנָה יְמֵי מִילָה, שִׁבְעָה יְמֵי שַׁבָּתָא, שִׁשָּׁה סִדְרֵי מִשְׁנָה, חֲמִשָּׁה חוּמְשֵׁי תוֹרָה, אַרְבַּע אִמָּהוֹת, שְׁלֹשָׁה אָבוֹת, שְׁנֵי לֻחוֹת הַבְּרִית, אֶחָד אֱלֹהֵינוּ שֶׁבַּשָּׁמַיִם וּבָאָרֶץ.

עֲשָׂרָה מִי יוֹדֵעַ? עֲשָׂרָה אֲנִי יוֹדֵעַ: עֲשָׂרָה דִבְּרַיָּא, תִּשְׁעָה יַרְחֵי לֵדָה, שְׁמוֹנָה יְמֵי מִילָה, שִׁבְעָה יְמֵי שַׁבָּתָא, שִׁשָּׁה סִדְרֵי מִשְׁנָה, חֲמִשָּׁה חוּמְשֵׁי תוֹרָה, אַרְבַּע אִמָּהוֹת, שְׁלֹשָׁה אָבוֹת, שְׁנֵי לֻחוֹת הַבְּרִית, אֶחָד אֱלֹהֵינוּ שֶׁבַּשָּׁמַיִם וּבָאָרֶץ.

אַחַד עָשָׂר מִי יוֹדֵעַ? אַחַד עָשָׂר אֲנִי יוֹדֵעַ: אַחַד עָשָׂר כּוֹכְבַיָּא, עֲשָׂרָה דִבְּרַיָּא, תִּשְׁעָה יַרְחֵי לֵדָה, שְׁמוֹנָה יְמֵי מִילָה, שִׁבְעָה יְמֵי שַׁבָּתָא, שִׁשָּׁה סִדְרֵי מִשְׁנָה, חֲמִשָּׁה חוּמְשֵׁי תוֹרָה, אַרְבַּע אִמָּהוֹת, שְׁלֹשָׁה אָבוֹת, שְׁנֵי לֻחוֹת הַבְּרִית, אֶחָד אֱלֹהֵינוּ שֶׁבַּשָּׁמַיִם וּבָאָרֶץ.

שְׁנֵים עָשָׂר מִי יוֹדֵעַ? שְׁנֵים עָשָׂר אֲנִי יוֹדֵעַ: שְׁנֵים עָשָׂר שִׁבְטַיָּא, אַחַד עָשָׂר כּוֹכְבַיָּא, עֲשָׂרָה דִבְּרַיָּא, תִּשְׁעָה יַרְחֵי לֵדָה, שְׁמוֹנָה יְמֵי מִילָה, שִׁבְעָה יְמֵי שַׁבָּתָא, שִׁשָּׁה סִדְרֵי מִשְׁנָה, חֲמִשָּׁה חוּמְשֵׁי תוֹרָה, אַרְבַּע אִמָּהוֹת, שְׁלֹשָׁה אָבוֹת, שְׁנֵי לֻחוֹת הַבְּרִית, אֶחָד אֱלֹהֵינוּ שֶׁבַּשָּׁמַיִם וּבָאָרֶץ.

שְׁלֹשָׁה עָשָׂר מִי יוֹדֵעַ? שְׁלֹשָׁה עָשָׂר אֲנִי יוֹדֵעַ: שְׁלֹשָׁה עָשָׂר מִדַּיָּא. שְׁנֵים עָשָׂר שִׁבְטַיָּא, אַחַד עָשָׂר כּוֹכְבַיָּא, עֲשָׂרָה דִבְּרַיָּא, תִּשְׁעָה יַרְחֵי לֵדָה, שְׁמוֹנָה

four are the mothers, three are the fathers, two are the tablets of the covenant, One is our God in the heavens and the earth.

CHAD GADYA

One kid, one kid (let's call him "little Jerry"[85]) that my father bought for two zuz, one kid, one kid.

Then came a **cat** and ate the kid that my father bought for two zuz, one kid, one kid. If this happened, maybe the dingo ate your baby![86]

Then came a **dog** and bit the cat, that ate the kid that my father bought for two zuz, one kid, one kid.

Then came a **stick** and hit the dog (better than dognapping it[87]), that bit the cat, that ate the kid that my father bought for two zuz, one kid, one kid.

Then came **fire** and burnt the stick, that hit the dog, that bit the cat, that ate the kid that my father bought for two zuz, one kid, one kid.

Then came **water** and extinguished the fire (yeah, in six games[88]), that drank the water, that extinguished the fire, that burnt the stick, that hit the dog, that bit the cat, that ate the kid that my father bought for two zuz, one kid, one kid.

Then came a **bull** and drank the water, that extinguished the fire, that burnt the stick, that hit the dog, that bit the cat, that

══ BEE BA DO DUM DUM, BUM BADUM BUM BUH, BAH DUH, BAH DAH DUM DUM, DUM DEDUM DUM DUM DUM DUM. BADA DO DUM DEDUM. ══

The Chains of Events

In life and history, sometimes small and seemingly insignificant things affect events down the road. This happens many times in *Seinfeld*. In "The Opposite[C152]," Elaine is enjoying her Jujyfruit, and because her mouth was full, she couldn't tell her boss that he left his handkerchief. He then blows his nose into. his hand. Trying to be nice, he is then not willing to shake the hand of a possible business

THE (UNOFFICIAL) SEINFELD HAGGADAH

יְמֵי מִילָה, שִׁבְעָה יְמֵי שַׁבָּתָא, שִׁשָּׁה סִדְרֵי מִשְׁנָה, חֲמִשָּׁה חוּמְשֵׁי תוֹרָה, אַרְבַּע אִמָּהוֹת, שְׁלֹשָׁה אָבוֹת, שְׁנֵי לֻחוֹת הַבְּרִית, אֶחָד אֱלֹהֵינוּ שֶׁבַּשָּׁמַיִם וּבָאָרֶץ.

חד גדיא

חַד גַּדְיָא, חַד גַּדְיָא דְּזַבִּין אַבָּא בִּתְרֵי זוּזֵי, חַד גַּדְיָא, חַד גַּדְיָא.

וְאָתָא שׁוּנְרָא וְאָכְלָה לְגַדְיָא, דְּזַבִּין אַבָּא בִּתְרֵי זוּזֵי. חַד גַּדְיָא, חַד גַּדְיָא.

וְאָתָא כַלְבָּא וְנָשַׁךְ לְשׁוּנְרָא, דְּאָכְלָה לְגַדְיָא, דְּזַבִּין אַבָּא בִּתְרֵי זוּזֵי. חַד גַּדְיָא, חַד גַּדְיָא.

וְאָתָא חוּטְרָא וְהִכָּה לְכַלְבָּא, דְּנָשַׁךְ לְשׁוּנְרָא, דְּאָכְלָה לְגַדְיָא, דְּזַבִּין אַבָּא בִּתְרֵי זוּזֵי. חַד גַּדְיָא, חַד גַּדְיָא.

וְאָתָא נוּרָא וְשָׂרַף לְחוּטְרָא, דְּהִכָּה לְכַלְבָּא, דְּנָשַׁךְ לְשׁוּנְרָא, דְּאָכְלָה לְגַדְיָא, דְּזַבִּין אַבָּא בִּתְרֵי זוּזֵי. חַד גַּדְיָא, חַד גַּדְיָא.

וְאָתָא מַיָּא וְכָבָה לְנוּרָא, דְּשָׂרַף לְחוּטְרָא, דְּהִכָּה לְכַלְבָּא, דְּנָשַׁךְ לְשׁוּנְרָא, דְּאָכְלָה לְגַדְיָא, דְּזַבִּין אַבָּא

בי בה דו דום דום, בום בדום בום בן, בה דו, בה דה דום דום, דום דדום דום דום דום. בדה דו דום דדום.

partner, which leads to the end of Pendant Publishing, and with it, Elaine's job. Elaine herself realizes the cause and effect: "Because they're Jujyfruit. I like them. I didn't know it would start a chain reaction that would lead to the end of Pendant Publishing."

In "The Junior Mint[C153]," Jerry and Kramer are invited to watch a surgery from the gallery. Kramer is insistent on both eating Junior Mints and giving one to Jerry. Kramer's actions make one mint fall

נרצה — 159

ate the kid that my father bought for two zuz, one kid, one kid.

Then came the **schochet** and slaughtered the bull (instead of running out and pushing people in the way[89]), that burnt the stick, that hit the dog, that bit the cat, that ate the kid that my father bought for two zuz, one kid, one kid.

Then came the **angel of death** and slaughtered the schochet, who slaughtered the bull, that drank the water, that extinguished the fire, that burnt the stick, that hit the dog, that bit the cat, that ate the kid that my father bought for two zuz, one kid, one kid.

Then came the **Holy One, blessed be He** and slaughtered the angel of death, who slaughtered the schochet, who slaughtered the bull, that drank the water, that extinguished the fire, that burnt the stick, that hit the dog, that bit the cat, that ate the kid that my father bought for two zuz, one kid, one kid.

═ BEE BA DO DUM DUM, BUM BADUM BUM BUH, BAH DUH, BAH DAH DUM DUM, DUM DEDUM DUM DUM DUM DUM. BADA DO DUM DEDUM. ═

into the patient, Elaine's boyfriend, Roy. The mint ends up saving Roy. The doctor does not realize what happened, so he says: " I have no medical evidence to back me up, but something happened during the operation that staved off that infection. Something beyond science. Something perhaps from above..."

In "The Marine Biologist[C154]," Jerry falsely mentions that George is a marine biologist to a woman they went to school with. During a walk on the beach, George and this woman see a beached whale. Still pretending he is a marine biologist, George tries to save the whale. During the rescue, he finds Kramer's golf ball in the blowhole of the great beast. A minor action by Kramer, hitting golf balls into the ocean, leads to George's stunning story. In these instances and so so many more, *Seinfeld* makes us believe that disparate events are part of a larger story.

We sing what appears to be a kids song at the end of the Seder, and there are many explanations of Chad Gadya's symbolism. What

THE (UNOFFICIAL) SEINFELD HAGGADAH

בִּתְרֵי זוּזֵי. חַד גַּדְיָא, חַד גַּדְיָא.

וְאָתָא תוֹרָא וְשָׁתָה לְמַיָּא, דְּכָבָה לְנוּרָא, דְּשָׂרַף לְחוּטְרָא, דְּהִכָּה לְכַלְבָּא, דְּנָשַׁךְ לְשׁוּנְרָא, דְּאָכְלָה לְגַדְיָא, דְּזַבִּין אַבָּא בִּתְרֵי זוּזֵי. חַד גַּדְיָא, חַד גַּדְיָא.

וְאָתָא הַשּׁוֹחֵט וְשָׁחַט לְתוֹרָא, דְּשָׁתָה לְמַיָּא, דְּכָבָה לְנוּרָא, דְּשָׂרַף לְחוּטְרָא, דְּהִכָּה לְכַלְבָּא, דְּנָשַׁךְ לְשׁוּנְרָא, דְּאָכְלָה לְגַדְיָא, דְּזַבִּין אַבָּא בִּתְרֵי זוּזֵי. חַד גַּדְיָא, חַד גַּדְיָא.

וְאָתָא מַלְאַךְ הַמָּוֶת וְשָׁחַט לְשׁוֹחֵט, דְּשָׁחַט לְתוֹרָא, דְּשָׁתָה לְמַיָּא, דְּכָבָה לְנוּרָא, דְּשָׂרַף לְחוּטְרָא, דְּהִכָּה לְכַלְבָּא, דְּנָשַׁךְ לְשׁוּנְרָא, דְּאָכְלָה לְגַדְיָא, דְּזַבִּין אַבָּא בִּתְרֵי זוּזֵי. חַד גַּדְיָא, חַד גַּדְיָא.

וְאָתָא הַקָּדוֹשׁ בָּרוּךְ הוּא וְשָׁחַט לְמַלְאַךְ הַמָּוֶת, דְּשָׁחַט לְשׁוֹחֵט, דְּשָׁחַט לְתוֹרָא, דְּשָׁתָה לְמַיָּא, דְּכָבָה לְנוּרָא, דְּשָׂרַף לְחוּטְרָא, דְּהִכָּה לְכַלְבָּא, דְּנָשַׁךְ לְשׁוּנְרָא, דְּאָכְלָה לְגַדְיָא, דְּזַבִּין אַבָּא בִּתְרֵי זוּזֵי. חַד גַּדְיָא, חַד גַּדְיָא.

===== בִּי בָּה דוּ דוּם דוּם, בּוּם בָּדוּם בּוּם בּוֹן, בָּה דוּ, בָּה דָּה דוּם דוּם, דוּם דָּדוּם דוּם דוּם דוּם. בָּדָה דוּ דוּם דוּם. =====

many of the explanations have in common is that there is a chain of events, starting from a metaphoric little baby goat that leads all the way up to God on top. Over the long Seder we discussed past and future redemptions. We end the Seder with an acknowledgement: that the large events in our lives, personal and communal, don't just happen. They are built on a chain of events starting from what one father decides to buy. That knowledge can give us both hope for a better future and the responsibility to create it, one bought baby goat at a time.

נרצה — 161

Appendix
Recipes if *Seinfeld* had a Seder

Yev Kaseem's (The "Soup Nazi") Chicken Soup
Published by Elaine Benes

Ingredients:
3 Parsnip
3 Carrot
2 Zucchini
½ a bunch of Dill
3 Chicken drumsticks or 4 wings
Salt, pepper, soup consommé

Instructions:
1. Peel and cut up (into small cubes) the parsnip, carrots, and zucchini
2. Wash and cut up the dill
3. Add the chicken
4. Fill with water and bring to a boil. Then let simmer on low.
5. Add spices for taste: salt, pepper, 4 TB of KFP soup consommé

Raquel Welch's Matzah Balls

Ingredients:
Matzah meal
3 Large Eggs
⅓ of a cup of Seltzer
¼ of a cup of preferred KFP vegetable oil
salt and pepper

Instructions:
1. Beat the 3 eggs
2. Add the seltzer and oil
3. Add matzah meal slowly until it is runny but not thick
4. Add salt and pepper to taste
5. Keep in fridge for one hour
6. Bring soup to boil, and scoop balls to preferred size into the soup

Mr. Lippman's Double Chocolate Muffin Tops

Ingredients:

½ cup matzah cake meal
6 Tablespoons potato starch
¾ cup sugar
¼ cup cocoa
¼ teaspoon salt
2 teaspoons baking powder*

1 teaspoon baking soda
⅔ cup nonfat yogurt
⅔ cup milk
1 egg, lightly beaten
1 package vanilla sugar or 1 teaspoon vanilla
1 cup chocolate chips

Instructions:

1. Mix together dry ingredients.
2. Mix together wet ingredients.
3. Blend the two mixtures just till moistened. Fold in chocolate chips.
4. Place in oiled or nonstick muffin tins.
5. Bake about 15 minutes at 400°F or till they test done with a toothpick.
6. Break off the top of the muffin
7. Do not make too many or it may be difficult to discard the stumps.

Jerry's Black and White Cookies

Ingredients:

1 cup matzah cake meal
2 Tbsp potato starch
½ tsp baking soda
½ tsp salt
½ cup margarine

½ cup white sugar
½ cup packed light brown sugar
1 large egg
1 ¼ cup semi-sweet chocolate chips

Instructions:

1. Mix all ingredients
2. Roll the dough into small walnut sized balls and place on a cookie sheet. Then, flatten the balls with the palm of your hand.
3. Bake on 375 for about 12 minutes or until golden brown.
4. Melt Chocolate (in a glass bowl above boiling water) and dip the cookies half way into the melted chocolate
5. If you have KFP white chocolate do the same thing on the other side of the cookie

Frank Costanza's Stuffed Cabbage

Ingredients:
1 large cabbage	⅓ cup brown sugar
½ cup dried quinoa	½ cup white wine
1 pound ground beef	Juice from 1 lemon
1 egg whisked	½ tablespoon cinnamon
2 garlic cloves	½ tablespoon parsley
¾ cup onion small diced	Salt and black pepper
42 ounce of crushed tomatoes	¼ teaspoon red pepper
½ cup onion small diced	

Instructions:
1. Fill a large pot with water and bring it to a boil. Boil cabbage in water until the leaves start to fall off and the cabbage darkens in color. Let cool.
2. While cabbage is cooling, mix together the filling. In a large bowl mix together cooked quinoa, beef, egg, garlic, ¾ cup onion, 1/3 cup crushed tomatoes, 1 teaspoon salt, and ¼ teaspoon black pepper. Set aside.
3. In a separate large bowl, mix together sauce ingredients. Mix diced tomatoes, remaining crushed tomatoes, ½ cup onion, brown sugar, white wine, lemon juice, cinnamon, parsley, 1 teaspoon salt and ½ teaspoon black pepper or to taste.
4. Once cabbage is cool, peel off 10-12 large leaves. Add about 4-5 tablespoons of filling near the bottom of the leaf. Fold the bottom over the filling, then fold in sides. Roll up like a burrito. Repeat with other leaves.
5. Pour about half the sauce onto the bottom of a pan, and top that with rolls. It's okay if the rolls overlap a bit. Pour remaining sauce on top. Bring mixture to a simmer, lower to low heat, cover, and cook for 90 minutes to two hours until cabbage is tender.
6. Let cool and refrigerate overnight. The next day, if the sauce is thin remove cabbage rolls and simmer sauce for about 10 minutes until reduced and thick.

Notes

Format: "Episode Title" Season #:Episode #

1. "The Red Dot" 3:12
2. "The Glasses" 5:3
3. "The Slicer" 9:7
4. "The Doodle" 6:20
5. "The Strike" 9:10
6. "The Summer of George" 8:22
7. "The Comeback" 8:13
8. "The Pie" 5:15
9. "The Note" 3:1
10. "The Reverse Peephole" 9:12
11. "The Stall" 5:12
12. "The Non-Fat Yogurt" 5:7
13. "The Pony Remark" 2:2
14. "The Deal" 2:13 and many others
15. "The Implant" 4:19
16. "The Trip" Part 1 4:1
17. "The Bizarro Jerry" 8:3
18. "The Chinese Woman" 6:4
19. "The Yada Yada" 8:19
20. "The Raincoats" 5:18
21. "The Lip Reader" 5:6
22. "The Pledge Drive" 6:3
23. "The Chinese Woman" 6:4
24. "The Puffy Shirt" 5:2
25. "The Sponge" 7:9
26. "The Alternate Side" 3:11
27. "The Millenium" 8:20
28. "The Doll" 7:16
29. "The Cafe" 3:7
30. "The Statue" 2:6
31. "The Gymnast" 6:6
32. "The Yada Yada" 8:19
33. "The Pen" 3:17
34. "The Chinese Woman" 6:4
35. "The Wink" 7:4
36. "The Engagement" 7:1
37. "The Alternate Side" 3:11
38. "The Suicide" 3:15
39. "The Gum" 7:10
40. "The Outing" 4:17
41. "The Big Salad" 6:2
42. "The Implant" 4:19
43. "The Fix-Up" 3:16
44. "The Apology" 9:9
45. "The Blood" 9:4
46. "The Parking Space" 3:22
47. "The Bookstore" 9:17
48. "The Bizarro Jerry" 8:3
49. "The Serenity Now" 9:3
50. "The Voice" 9:2
51. "The Pie" 5:15
52. "The Puffy Shirt" 5:2
53. "The Red Dot" 3:12
54. "The Dinner Party" 5:14
55. "The Frogger" 9:18
56. "The Doodle" 6:20
57. "The Smelly Car" 4:21
58. "The Conversion" 5:11
59. "The Old Man" 4:18
60. "The Junior Mint" 4:20
61. "The Heart Attack" 2:8, "The Suicide" 3:15
62. "The Parking Garage" 3:8
63. "The Invitations" 7:24
64. "The Pledge Drive" 6:3
65. "The Opera" 4:9
66. "The Library" 3:5
67. "The Yada Yada" 8:19
68. "The Wink" 7:4
69. "The Fusilli Jerry" 6:21
70. "The Airport" 4:12
71. "The Keys" 3:23
72. "The Marine Biologist" 5:14
73. "The Little Kicks" 8:4
74. "The Rye" 7:11
75. "The Soup" 6:7
76. "The Van Buren Boys" 8:14
77. "The Fatigues" 8:6
78. "The Strike 9:10
79. "The Marine Biologist" 5:14
80. "The Dinner Party" 5:13
81. "The Susie" 8:15
82. "The Chicken Roaster" 8:8
83. "The Secret Code" 7:7
84. "The Seven" 7:13
85. "The Little Jerry" 8:11
86. "The Stranded" 3:10
87. "The Dog" 3:4
88. "The Abstinence" 8:9
89. "The Fire" 5:20

Notes on Commentary

Format: "Episode Title" Season #:Episode #

C1	"The Pilot" 4:23	C46	"The Pie" 5:15
C2	"The Chinese Restaurant" 2:11	C47	"The Apology" 9:9
C3	"The Parking Garage" 3:6	C48	"The Pledge Drive" 6:3
C4	"The Non-Fat Yogurt" 5:7	C49	"The Postponement" 7:2
C5	"The Pilot" 4:23	C50	"The Beard" 6:16
C6	"The Finale" 9:23	C51	"The Dinner Party" 5:13
C7	"The Pilot" 4:23	C52	"The English Patient" 8:17
C8	"The Bizarro Jerry" 8:3	C53	"The Lip Reader" 5:6
C9	"The Watch" 4:6	C54	"The Sniffling Accountant" 5:4
C10	"The Engagement" 7:1	C55	"The Pony Remark" 2:2
C11	"The Phone Message" 2:4	C56	"The Cadillac" 7:15
C12	"The Strike" 9:10	C57	"The Bizarro Jerry" 8:3
C13	"The Sponge" 7:9	C58	"The Pool Guy" 7:8
C14	"The Engagement" 7:1	C59	"The Bookstore" 9:17
C15	"The Pothole" 8:16	C60	"The Bizarro Jerry" 8:3
C16	"The Bubble Boy" 4:7	C61	"TThe Opposite" 5:22
C17	"The Puffy Shirt" 5:2	C62	"The Abstinence" 8:9
C18	"The Bubble Boy" 4:7	C63	"The Big Salad" 6:2
C19	"The Cheever Letters" 4:8	C64	"The Implant" 4:19
C20	"The Wallet" 4:5	C65	"The Yada Yada" 8:19
C21	"The Pen" 3:3	C66	"The Yada Yada" 8:19
C22	"The Van Buren Boys" 8:14	C67	"The Label Maker" 6:12
C23	"The Wallet" 4:5	C68	"The Raincoats" 5:18
C24	"The Wizard" 9:15	C69	"The Serenity Now" 9:3
C25	"The Wallet" 4:5	C70	"The Contest" 4:11
C26	"The Finale" 9:23	C71	"The Phone Message" 2:4
C27	"The Betrayal" 9:8	C72	"The Apartment" 2:5
C28	"The Suicide" 3:15	C73	"The Nose Job" 3:9
C29	"The Cadillac" 7:14	C74	"The Kiss Hello" 6:17
C30	"The Suicide" 3:15	C75	"The Cartoon" 9:13
C31	"The Serenity Now" 9:3	C76	"The Finale 9:23
C32	"The Opposite" 5:2	C77	"The Millenium" 8:20
C33	"The Chicken Roaster" 8:8	C78	"The Lip Reader" 5:6
C34	"The Soup Nazi" 7:6	C79	"The Old Man" 4:18
C35	"The Non-Fat Yogurt" 5:7	C80	"The Masseuse" 5:9
C36	"The Calzones" 7:20	C81	"The Nose Job" 3:9
C37	"The Comeback" 8:13	C82	"The Cadillac" 7:14
C38	"The Rye" 7:11	C83	"The Secret Code" 7:7
C39	"The Dinner Party" 5:13	C84	"The Cafe" 3:7
C40	"The Reverse Peephole" 9:12	C85	"The Butter Shave" 9:1
C41	"The Nap" 8:18	C86	"The Sniffling Accountant" 5:4
C42	"The Finale" 9:23	C87	"The Engagement" 7:1
C43	"The Non-Fat Yogurt" 5:7	C88	"The Deal" 2:9
C44	"The Doodle" 6:20	C89	"The Deal" 2:9
C45	"The Voice" 9:2	C90	"The Opposite" 5:22

Notes on Commentary (continued)
Format: "Episode Title" Season #:Episode #

C91 "The Alternate Side" 3:11
C92 "The Visa" 4:15
C93 "The Seinfeld Chronicles" 1:1
C94 "The Fix Up" 3:16
C95 "The Mom and Pop Store" 6:8
C96 "The Big Salad" 6:2
C97 "The Summer of George" 8:22
C98 "The Seinfeld Chronicles" 1:1
C99 "The Ex-Girlfriend" 2:1
C100 "The Pez Dispenser" 3:14
C101 "The Keys" 3:23
C102 "The Chicken Roaster" 8:8
C103 "The Blood" 9:4
C104 "The Fix Up" 3:16
C105 "The Mom and Pop Store" 6:8
C106 "The Chaperone" 6:1
C107 "The Boyfriend" 3:17
C108 "The Stock Tip" 1:5
C109 "The Gum" 7:10
C110 "The Invitations" 7:24
C111 "The Trip" 4:2
C112 "The Soup Nazi" 7:6
C113 "The Baby Shower 2:10
C114 "The Raincoats" 5:18
C115 "The Pledge Drive" 6:3
C116 "The Merv Griffin Show" 9:6
C117 "The Soup Nazi" 7:6
C118 "The Face Painter" 6:23
C119 "The Soup" 6:7
C120 "The Fatigues" 8:6
C121 "The Chicken Roaster" 8:8
C122 "The Fix Up" 3:16
C123 "The Chicken Roaster" 8:8
C124 "The Visa" 4:15
C125 "The Voice" 9:2
C126 "The Alternate Side" 3:11
C127 "The Keys" 3:23
C128 "The Pick" 4:13; "The Letter" 3:20; "The Abstinance" 8:9
C129 "The Trip" 4:1
C130 "The Cigar Store Indian" 5:10
C131 "The Couch" 6:5
C132 "The Pool Guy" 7:8
C133 "The Burning" 9:16
C134 "The Package" 8:5
C135 "The English Patient" 8:17
C136 "The Bookstore" 8:17
C137 "The Strike" 9:10
C138 "The Millenium" 8:20
C139 "The Muffin Tops" 8:21
C140 Ibid
C141 "The Bizarro Jerry" 8:3
C142 "The Shower Head" 7:16
C143 "The Robbery" 1:3
C144 "The Subway" 3:13 (and more)
C145 "The Andrea Doria" 8:10
C146 "The Mango" 5:1
C147 "The Kiss Hello" 6:17
C148 "The Chaperone" 6:1
C149 "The Package" 8:5
C150 "The Millenium" 8:20
C151 "The Boyfriend" 3:17
C152 "The Opposite" 5:22
C153 "The Junior Mint" 4:20
C154 "The Marine Biologist" 5:14

Manufactured by Amazon.ca
Bolton, ON